The Aqua

PISCES

Bernard Fitzwalter has been interested in astrology since he was about six, when he played King Herod's astrologer in his primary school nativity play. For the past six years he has been teaching astrology for the Marylebone-Paddington Institute, and for seven years he has had a regular column in OVER 21 magazine. In 1984 he appeared in the first series of Anglia Television's *Zodiac Game*, which prompted the *Daily Mirror* to say that he was 'enough to give astrology a good name'.

AQUARIAN SUN SIGN GUIDES

PISCES

20 FEBRUARY ~ 20 MARCH

Bernard Fitzwalter

Cover illustration by Steinar Lund
Cover typography by Steven Lee

THE AQUARIAN PRESS
Wellingborough, Northamptonshire

First published 1987

British Library Cataloguing in Publication Data

Fitzwalter, Bernard
Pisces.—(The Aquarian sun sign guides)
1. Zodiac
1. Title
133.5'4   BF1728.A2

ISBN 0-85030-583-7

*The Aquarian Press is part of the
Thorsons Publishing Group*

Printed and bound in Great Britain

Contents

PART 4: PISCES TRIVIA

Introduction

This book has been written to help you find out a little about astrology and a lot about yourself. It explains, for the first time, the motives and aims that guide your actions and make you do things the way you do; what it does not do is give you a list of 'typical Pisces' things to see if you recognize any of them. You are not likely to be typical anything: you are unique. What you *do* have in common with others who have birthdays at about the same time as you is a way of using your energy, a way of thinking, a set of motives and beliefs which seem to make sense to you, and which other people, those of the other eleven signs, obviously do not have. This book shows you those motives and beliefs, and shows you how they fit in with those of the other eleven signs. The zodiac is like a jigsaw: all the pieces have to be there for the whole picture to emerge.

This book also sets out to answer some very simple questions which are often asked but seldom answered. Questions like 'Why does the zodiac have twelve signs?' and 'What does being a Pisces actually mean?' as well as 'Why are Pisceans supposed to be indecisive? Why can't they be firm instead?' and 'Why don't all the people of the same star sign look the same.?'

The reason that these questions are seldom answered is because all too many astrologers don't know the rudiments of astrological theory, and what they do know they don't tell, because they think it is too difficult for the man in the street to understand. This is obvious nonsense: astrology was devised for and by people who did not normally read or write as much as we do, nor did they all have PhDs or the equivalent. The man in the street is quite capable of understanding anything provided that it is shown simply and clearly, from first principles upwards, and provided he has sufficient interest. Buying this book is evidence enough of your interest, and I hope that the explanations are simple enough and clear enough for you. If they are not, it is my fault, and not that of astrology.

How to Use this Book

The book is in four parts. It is best to read them in sequence, but if you have neither time nor patience, then they each work individually. Part 2 does not assume that you have read Part 1, though it helps. Part 3 makes a lot more sense if you have already read Parts 1 and 2, but it isn't mandatory. Part 4, although just as firmly based on astrological principles as the other three, is deliberately intended as light relief.

The first part of the book deals with the theory behind the zodiac; it sets out the principles of astrology and enables you to see why Pisces is assigned the qualities it has, how the ruling planet system works, and what all the other signs are like in terms of motivation, so you can compare them to your own. There is a short and effective method given for assessing the aims and motives of other people. When you read Part 3 you will need to know a bit about the other signs, as you will be finding out that you have more to you than just the Pisces part you knew about.

The second part describes the essential Pisces. It shows you how there are different sorts of Pisceans according to where your birthday falls in the month, and shows how Piscean energy is used differently in the Pisces as a child, adult, and parent.

Since you spend the greatest part of your life in dealing with other individuals, the way Pisces deals with relationships is treated in some detail. This is the largest section of the book.

The third part shows you a different kind of zodiac, and

enables you to go into your own life in much greater detail. It isn't complicated, but you do need to think. It crosses the border between the kind of astrology you get in the magazines, and the sort of thing a real astrologer does. There's no reason why you can't do it yourself because, after all, you know yourself best.

The fourth part shows you the surface of being a Pisces, and how that zodiacal energy comes out in your clothes, your home, even your favourite food. The final item of this part actually explains the mechanics of being lucky, which you probably thought was impossible.

I hope that when you finished reading you will have a clearer view of yourself, and maybe like yourself a little more. Don't throw the book away; read it again in a few months' time—you will be surprised at what new thoughts about yourself it prompts you to form!

A Final Note

Throughout this book, the pronouns 'he', 'him', and 'his' have been used to describe both male and female. Everything which applies to a male Piscean applies to a female Piscean as well. There are two reasons why I have not bothered to make the distinction: firstly, to avoid long-windedness; secondly, because astrologically there is no need. It is not possible to tell from a horoscope whether the person to whom it relates is male or female, because to astrology they are both living individuals full of potential.

BERNARD FITZWALTER

Part 1

How the Zodiac Works

1. The Meaning of the Zodiac

Two Times Two is Four; Four Times Three is Twelve

It is no accident that there are twelve signs in the zodiac,
although there are a great many people who reckon themselves
to be well versed in astrology who do not know the reasons why,
and cannot remember ever having given thought to the principles
behind the circle of twelve.

The theory is quite simple, and once you are familiar with it, it
will enable you to see the motivation behind all the other signs
as well as your own. What's more, you only have to learn nine
words to do it. That's quite some trick—being able to understand
what anybody else you will ever meet is trying to do, with nine
words.

It works like this.

The zodiac is divided into twelve signs, as you know. Each of
the twelve represents a stage in the life cycle of solar energy as it
is embodied in the life of mankind here on our planet. There are
tides in this energy; sometimes it flows one way, sometimes
another, like the tides of the ocean. Sometimes it is held static, in
the form of an object, and sometimes it is released when that
object is broken down after a period of time. The twelve signs
show all these processes, both physical and spiritual, in their
interwoven pattern.

Six signs are used to show the flowing tide, so to speak, and six for the ebbing tide. Aries, Gemini, Leo, Libra, Sagittarius, and Aquarius are the 'flowing' group, and the others form the second group. You will notice at once that the signs alternate, one with the other, around the zodiac, so that the movement is maintained, and there is never a concentration of one sort of energy in one place. People whose Sun sign is in the first group tend to radiate their energies outwards from themselves. They are the ones who like to make the first move, like to be the ones to take command of a situation, like to put something of themselves into whatever they are doing. They don't feel right standing on the sidelines; they are the original have-a-go types. Energy comes out of them and is radiated towards other people, in the same way as the Sun's energy is radiated out to the rest of the solar system.

The people in the other signs are the opposite to that, as you would expect. They collect all the energy from the first group, keeping it for themselves and making sure none is wasted. They absorb things from a situation or from a personal contact, rather than contributing to it. They prefer to watch and learn rather than make the first move. They correspond to the Moon, which collects and reflects the energy of the Sun. One group puts energy out, one group takes it back in. The sun total of energy in the universe remains constant, and the two halves of the zodiac gently move to and fro with the tide of the energies.

This energy applies both to the real and concrete world of objects, as well as to the intangible world of thoughts inside our heads.

A distinction has to be made, then, between the real world and the intangible world. If this is done, we have four kinds of energy: outgoing and collecting, physical and mental. These four kinds of energy have been recognized for a long time, and were given names to describe the way they work more than two thousand years ago. These are the elements. All the energy in the cosmos can be described in the terms of these four: Fire, Earth, Air, Water.

Fire is used to describe that outgoing energy which applies to the real and physical world. There are three signs given to it: Aries, Leo, and Sagittarius. People with the Sun in any of these signs find themselves with the energy to get things going. They are at their best when making a personal contribution to a situation, and they expect to see some tangible results for their efforts. They are sensitive to the emotional content of anything, but that is not their prime concern, and so they tend to let it look after itself while they busy themselves with the actual matter in hand. Wherever you meet Fire energy in action, it will be shown as a person whose personal warmth and enthusiasm is having a direct effect on his surroundings.

Earth is used to describe the real and physical world where the energies are being collected and stored, sometimes in the form of material or wealth. The three signs given to the element are Taurus, Virgo, and Capricorn. Where Fire energy in people makes them want to move things, Earth energy makes them want to hold things and stop them moving. The idea of touching and holding, and so that of possession, is important to these people, and you can usually see it at work in the way they behave towards their own possessions. The idea is to keep things stable, and to hold energy stored for some future time when it will be released. Earth Sun people work to ensure that wherever they are is secure and unlikely to change; if possible they would like the strength and wealth of their situation to increase, and will work towards that goal. Wherever you meet Earth energy in action, there will be more work being done than idle chat, and there will be a resistance to any kind of new idea. There will be money being made, and accumulated. The idea of putting down roots and bearing fruit may be a useful one to keep in mind when trying to understand the way this energy functions.

Air is used to describe outgoing mental energies; put more simply, this is communication. Here the ideas are formed in the mind of the individual, and put out in the hope that they can influence and meet the ideas of another individual; this is communication, in an abstract sense. Gemini, Libra, and Aquarius are all Air signs, and people with the Sun in those signs are very much concerned with communicating their energies to others. Whether anything gets done as a result of all the conversation is not actually important; if there is to be a concrete result, then that is the province of Fire or Earth energies. Here the emphasis is on shaping the concept, not the reality. There is an affinity with Fire energies, because both of them are outgoing, but other than that they do not cross over into each other's territory. Wherever you meet Air energy in action, there is a lot of talk, and new ideas are thrown up constantly, but there is no real or tangible result, no real product, and no emotional involvement; were there to be emotional content, the energies would be watery ones.

Water is the collection of mental energies. It is the response to communication or action. It absorbs and dissolves everything else, and puts nothing out. In a word, it is simply feelings. Everything emotional is watery by element, because it is a response to an outside stimulus, and is often not communicated. It is not, at least not in its pure sense, active or initiatory, and it does not bring anything into being unless transformed into energy of a different type, such as Fire. Cancer, Scorpio and Pisces are the Water signs, and natives of those signs are often moody, withdrawn, and uncommunicative. Their energy collects the energy of others, and keeps their mental responses to external events stored. They are not being sad for any particular reason; it is simply the way that energy works. It is quite obvious that they are not showing an outgoing energy, but neither have they anything tangible to show for their efforts, like the money and property which seems to accumulate around Earth people. Water people simply absorb, keep to themselves, and do not communicate. To the onlooker, this appears unexciting, but there again the onlooker is biased: Fire and Air energies only appreciate outgoing energy forms, Earth energies recognize material rather than mental energies, and other Water energies are staying private and self-contained!

We now recognize four kinds of energy. Each of these comes in three distinct phases; if one zodiac sign is chosen to represent each of these phases within an element, there would be twelve different kinds of energy, and that would define the zodiac of twelve, with each one showing a distinct and different phase of the same endless flow of energy.

The first phase, not surprisingly, is a phase of definition, where the energies take that form for the first time, and where they are at their purest; they are not modified by time or circumstance, and what they aim to do is to start things in their own terms. These four most powerful signs (one for each element, remember) are called cardinal signs: Aries, Cancer, Libra, Capricorn. When the Sun enters any of these signs, the seasons change; the first day of the Sun's journey through Aries is the first day of spring, and the Spring equinox; Libra marks the Autumnal equinox, while Cancer and Capricorn mark Mid-summer's Day and the shortest day respectively.

The second phase is where the energy is mature, and spreads itself a little; it is secure in its place, and the situation is well established, so there is a sort of thickening and settling of the energy flow. Here it is at its most immobile, even Air. The idea is one of maintenance and sustenance, keeping things going and keeping them strong. This stage is represented by Taurus, Leo, Scorpio, and Aquarius, and they are called, unsurprisingly, fixed signs. These four signs, and their animal symbols, are often taken to represent the four winds and the four directions North, South, East and West. Their animal symbols (with an eagle instead of a scorpion for Scorpio) turn up all over Europe as tokens for the evangelists Luke, Mark, John and Matthew (in that order).

The final phase is one of dissolution and changes, as the energy finds itself applied to various purposes, and in doing so is changed into other forms. There is an emphasis on being used for the good, but being used up nonetheless. The final four signs are Gemini, Virgo, Sagittarius, and Pisces; in each of them the energies of their element are given back out for general use and benefit from where they had been maintained in the fixed phase. It is this idea of being used and changed which leads to this phase being called mutable.

Three phases of energy, then; one to form, one to grow strong and mature, and one to be used, and to become, at the end, something else. Like the waxing, full, and waning phases of the Moon.

The diagram below shows the twelve signs arranged in their sequence round the zodiac. Notice how cleverly the cycle and phases interweave:

(a) Outgoing and collecting energies alternate, with no two the same next to each other;

(b) Physical ebb and flow are followed by mental ebb and flow alternately in pairs round the circle, meaning that the elements follow in sequence round the circle three times;

(c) Cardinal, fixed, and mutable qualities follow in sequence round the circle four times, and yet

(d) No two elements or qualities the same are next to each other, even though their sequences are not broken.

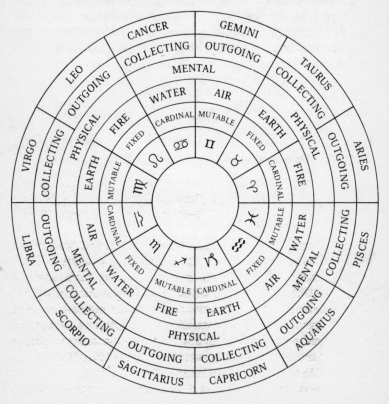

The interweaving is perfect. The zodiac shows all forms of energy, physical and mental, outgoing or incoming, waxing or waning, harmoniously forming a perfectly balanced unity when all the components are taken together. Humanity, as a whole, contains all the possibilities; each individual is a component necessary to the whole.

All this can be a bit long-winded when what you want is some way of holding all that information for instant recall and use, which is where the nine words come in.

If a single word is used for the kind of energy flow, and another two for the element and quality, then they can be used to form a sentence which will describe the way the energy is being used.

As a suggestion (use other words if they are more meaningful to you), try 'outgoing' and 'collecting' for the energy flows.

Next, for the elements:

Fire :	activity	(Aries, Leo, Sagittarius)
Earth :	material	(Taurus, Virgo, Capricorn)
Air :	communication	(Gemini, Libra, Aquarius)
Water :	feelings	(Cancer, Scorpio, Pisces)

And for the qualities:

Cardinal :	defining	(Aries, Cancer, Libra, Capricorn)
Fixed :	maintaining	(Taurus, Leo, Scorpio, Aquarius)
Mutable :	using	(Gemini, Virgo, Sagittarius, Pisces)

Now in answer to the question 'What is a Gemini doing?' and answer can be formed as 'He's outgoing, and he's using communication', which neatly encapsulates the motivation of the sign. All that you need to know about the guiding principles of a Gemini individual, no matter who he is, is in that sentence. He will never deviate from that purpose, and you can adapt your own actions to partner or oppose his intention as you please.

A Scorpio? He's collecting, and he's maintaining his feelings. An Arian? He's outgoing, and he's defining activity. And so on. Those nine words, or some similar ones which you like better, can be used to form effective and useful phrases which describe the motivation of everybody you will ever meet. How different people show it is their business, but their motivation and purpose is clear if you know their birthday.

Remember, too, that this motivation works at all levels, from the immediate to the eternal. The way a Taurean conducts himself in today's problems is a miniature of the way he is trying to achieve his medium-term ambitions over the next two or three years. It is also a miniature of his whole existence: when, as an old man, he looks back to see what he tried to do and what he achieved, both the efforts and the achievement, whatever it is, can be described in the same phrase with the same three words.

2. The Planets and the Horseshoe

You will have heard, or read, about the planets in an astrological context. You may have a horoscope in a magazine which says that Mars is here or Jupiter is there, and that as a consequence this or that is likely to happen to you. Two questions immediately spring to mind: What do the planets signify? How does that affect an individual?

The theory is straightforward again, and not as complex as that of the zodiac signs in the previous chapter. Remember that the basic theory of astrology is that since the universe and mankind are part of the same Creation, they both move in a similar fashion, so Man's movements mirror those of the heavens. So far, so good. If you look at the sky, night after night, or indeed day after day, it looks pretty much the same; the stars don't move much in relationship to each other, at least not enough to notice. What do move, though, are the Sun and Moon, and five other points of light—the planets. It must therefore follow that if these are the things which move, they must be the things which can be related to the movements of Man. Perhaps, the theory goes, they have areas of the sky in which they feel more at home, where the energy that they represent is stronger; there might be other places where they are uncomfortable and weak, corresponding to the times in your life when you just can't win no matter what you do. The planets would then behave like ludo counters, moving round the heavens trying to get back to a home of their own colour, and then starting a new game.

The scheme sounds plausible, makes a sort of common sense, and is endearingly human; all hallmarks of astrological thought, which unlike scientific thought has to relate everything to the human experience. And so it is: the planets are given values to show the universal energy in different forms, and given signs of the zodiac as homes. Therefore you Sun sign also has a planet to look after it, and the nature of that planet will show itself strongly in your character.

The planets used are the Sun and Moon, which aren't really planets at all, one being a satellite and the other a star, and then Mercury, Venus, Mars, Jupiter, and Saturn. This was enough until the eighteenth century, when Uranus was discovered, followed in the subsequent two hundred years by Neptune and P luto. Some modern astrologers put the three new planets into horoscopes, but it really isn't necessary, and may not be such a good idea anyway. There are three good reasons for this:

(a)   The modern planets break up the symmetry of the original system, which was perfectly harmonious;

(b)   The old system is still good enough to describe everything that can happen in a human life, and the modern planets have little to add;

(c)   Astrology is about the relationship between the sky and a human being. An ordinary human being cannot see the outer planets on his own; he needs a telescope. We should leave out of the system such things as are of an extra-human scale or magnitude: they do not apply to an ordinary human. If we put in things which are beyond ordinary human capabilities, we cannot relate them to the human experience, and we are wasting our time.

In the diagram on page 21, the zodiac is presented in its usual form, but it has also been split into two from the start of Leo to the start of Aquarius. The right hand half is called the solar half, and the other one is the lunar half. The Sun is assigned to Leo because in the Northern hemisphere, where astrology started, August is when you feel the influence of the Sun most, especially in the Eastern Mediterranean, where the Greeks and the other early Western civilizations were busy putting the framework of astrology together in the second millenium BC. The Sun is important because it gives light. The Moon gives light too; it is reflected sunlight, but it is enough to see by, and this is enough to give the Sun and Moon the title of 'the Lights' in astrology. The Moon is assigned to Cancer, so that the two of them can balance and complement each other. From there, moving away from the Lights around the circle on both sides, the signs have the planets assigned to them starting with the fastest mover, Mercury, and continuing in decreasing order of speed. Saturn is the slowest mover of all, and the two signs opposite to

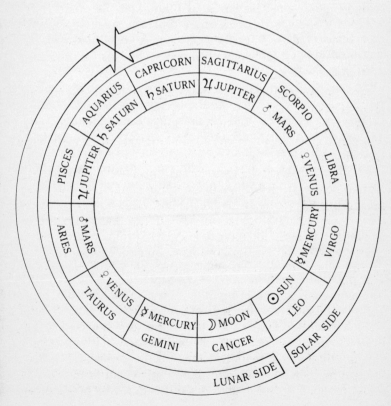

the Lights are both governed by that planet. The reasons for this apparent assymmetry will be explained in a little while. This arrangement is, of course, the horseshoe of the title to this chapter.

The Sun and Moon work in a similar fashion to the outgoing and collecting energies we noted earlier with the twelve signs. The Sun is radiant above all else; energy comes outwards from it, warming and energizing all those around it. Leo people, whose sign is the Sun's, work like this by being at the centre of a group of people and acting as inspiration and encouragement to them all. The Moon reflects the Sun's light, and energies of a lunar kind are directed inwards towards the core of the person. The two energies are necessarily linked; lunar people would starve without the solar folks' warmth, but the solar types need someone to radiate to or their purpose is unfulfilled.

The planets on each side of the horseshoe display their own pattern they are on.

Mercury and Venus form a pair, representing complementary but opposite ideas, which should be familiar by now. Mercury represents difference, and Venus stands for similarity.

Wherever anything new forms that is distinguishable from the background, then Mercury is there making it what it is, highlighting what makes it different. Anything separate is Mercurial, and words, since they are separate and can be strung together into millions of different combinations, are Mercurial too. Mercury is not a long-term influence; it notes things as being different for an instant, and then they become part of the establishment, and something else is new elsewhere. Because 'new' is an instantaneous state—that is, something can only be new once, and for a moment—Mercury is not associated with anything lasting, and its rapid motion as a planet leads to its being associated with the idea of speed. Virgo, Mercury's solar sign, is concerned with the changing of the shape of things ('collecting, using material' in our keyword system), while Gemini, the lunar sign, is concerned with reading and writing, and getting new ideas ('outgoing, using communication').

Venus does the reverse; it looks for that which is similar,

finding points of contact to make relationships between common interests and energies. It likes to preserve the harmonies of life, and resents anything which might interrupt them. Love and affection are naturally Venusian, but so is music and all of the Arts, for the harmonies they contain. Expressed in a solar way, Venus is Libra, the maker of relationships; its lunar face is Taurus, emphasizing food and furnishings as things which give pleasure to the individual.

The next pair are Mars and Jupiter. Mars applies force from the outside to impose structure on a disordered universe, while Jupiter expands forcibly from the inside to give growth and wealth, inviting everyone else to join in.

Mars is pure force, energy in a straight line with a direction to go in. Anger and passion are both Martian, and so is lust, because they are all examples of great energy directed towards a given end. Note that Martian force is not necessarily strength, wealth, or know-how, just pure energy, which often boils over and needs controlling. Mars is the power in an athlete, and in an assassin too. It is also the power in a lover, because the urge to create is also the urge to pro-create, and if that energy fulfils its purpose then that creation takes place. Scorpio is its solar side, the power to control and create; in lunar form it is shown by Aries, as energy enjoyed for its own sake by its owner, with no purpose except to express it.

Jupiter is the spirit of expansion from within; not only does it oppose Mars' force from outside, it opposes Mars' physicality with its own mental emphasis. Jupiter develops the mind, then. As it does so, it develops all natural talents of an academic nature, and encourages movement, enquiry and travel to broaden experience and knowledge. The Solar expression of this is Sagittarius, where the centaur symbol is both a wise teacher and a free-roaming wild horse at the same time. Jupiter in a lunar sense is Pisces, where the imagination is developed to a greater extent than anywhere else, but used to provide an internal dream world for the owner's pleasure. Great sensitivity here, but the lunar energies are not of the sort to be expressed; rather other energies are *im*pressed on the Piscean mind.

Saturn is the last of the five planets. He stands alone, and if it is necessary to consider him as paired with anything it is with the Lights as an entity together. The Lights are at the centre of the system; Saturn is at its edge. They are the originators of the energies of the zodiac, and he is the terminator. Everything to do with limits and ends is his. He represents Time, and lots of it, in contrast to Mercury, which represented the instant. He represents the sum total of all things, and the great structures and frameworks of long-term endeavour. In solar form he is Capricorn, the representative of hard work, all hierarchies, and all rulers; in lunar form he is Aquarius, showing the horizontal structure of groups of people within society at different levels. Here he denies the activity of Mars, because society is too big for one person to change against the collective will, and he contains the expansion of Jupiter within himself. Venus and Mercury can neither relate to it nor make it change, because it is always the same, in the end.

The planets show important principles in action, the same as the zodiac does. You have probably noticed that the horseshoe of the planets and the ring of the zodiac say the same thing in a different way, and that is true about most things in astrology. It may be that the two systems interrelate and overlap because they are from the same source: after all, $3+2+2=7$, which is the planet's total, and $3x2x2=12$, which is the signs'. How you assign the elements and qualities, pairs of planets and lights is for you to decide. The joy of astrology, like all magic, is that it has you at the centre, and is made to fit its user's requirements. Now you know the principles, you can use it as you please, and as it seems relevant to you.

Part 2

Yourself—and Others

3. The Essential Pisces

All the energy in the zodiac is solar, but that solar energy takes many forms. It is moderated and distributed through the planetary energies until it finally shows in you, the individual. For a Pisces, the prime planetary energy is that of Jupiter; you will be motivated by, and behave in the manner of, the energies of Jupiter. To remind yourself of what that means, read the section on Jupiter on page 23. As a sign of the zodiac, Pisces is a Mutable Water sign. Remind yourself what that means by reading page 17. Now we have to see how those essential principles work when expressed through a person and his motivation.

What it Means to be a Pisces

You know what it is to be a Pisces, because you are one; but you probably don't know what it is that makes a Pisces the way he is, because you cannot stand outside yourself. You would have to be each of the other eleven signs in turn to understand the nature of the energy that motivates you. This essential energy is in every Piscean, but it shows itself to different extents and in different ways. Because it is in every single Piscean, it is universal rather than specific, and universal ideas tend to come in language which sounds a little on the woolly side. You will think that it isn't really about what makes you who you are, because you don't feel like that every day—or at least you think you don't. In fact, you feel like that all the time, but you don't notice it any more than you notice your eyes focusing, yet they do it all the time, and you see things the way you do because of it.

The first thing to note is that the zodiac is a circle, not a line with a beginning and an end. If it were a line, then Pisces would be at the far end of it, but that would be to miss the point; if the zodiac is a circle, then Pisces is a stage in an endlessly repeating cycle, and we will get a much better idea of what it is if we look to see where it came from, and where it is going.

The sign before Pisces is Aquarius, Aquarius represents the energy present in groups of people gathered together for some common purpose. Earlier zodiac signs were concerned with the energy of the individual, first on his own, and later in contact with his immediate family and friends. By the time the zodiac has reached Aquarius, the circle of acquaintances has grown very large indeed—large enough for the energy of the sign to work best in the ideals that are held by a huge number of people. Pisces deals with a realm even bigger yet.

Imagine that. Imagine the energy that drives a single person, and keeps him alive. Extend its sphere of influence outwards, so that it becomes the energy that keeps a family together, the special warmth that makes a house a home. Extend it further, make it grow; it will go forwards in time through a person's children, and outwards in space to his circle of friends. Expand it into a whole society: now the energy is the structure of position and influence we all know so well, with the managing director at the top, and the tea-boy at the bottom. Now lift the energy above the physical level, so that it becomes the beliefs and hopes of all large groups of people, the shared enthusiasm that cuts across the structures of class and position. Where does the energy go from here? Is there anywhere further for it to expand?

Yes, there is, and that final stage is what Pisces is about. Until now the energy has been held in various forms; either the form of an individual, or within the limits of a defined group, such as a family or a nation. The final stage of the process (Pisces is the twelfth sign of the twelve) is where the energy goes beyond all forms and functions, to take in literally everything. The world of the Piscean contains everything that there has been so far, both in the real world and the world of the imagination. It contains all the feelings and ideas, all the emotions and inspiration that the universe contains. Everything is possible in the world of the Piscean, but nothing is definite. His world is without limits, but it is also without form.

Can you remember what a new packet of plasticine looked like, when you were a child? All the colours were clear and separate, but by the time you had finished playing with it, it was all the same colour, somehow. You knew that all the separate colours were in there somewhere, and that they had all contributed to what you had in front of you, but nothing was definite and identifiable any more. Pisces is like that final stage—it contains everything, but nothing is definite.

It sounds rather difficult to comprehend, doesn't it? How an individual Piscean can find some sort of reality for himself from such an impossibly vague and unformed universe is a difficult question. If you recognize the idea of the ocean of infinite possibility from your own life, as you should if you are Piscean, then you have most probably already made some sort of attempt at solving the problem.

Perhaps some sort of key can be found if we look at what comes after Pisces. The answer is, of course, Aries again, since the zodiac is an endless circle. Aries is the point at which something definite comes into being; where something coalesces from the infinite possibilities of the Piscean stage, and becomes actual instead of theoretical. In due time, of course, whatever it was that formed in its Arian phase will develop and expand through the phases of the other signs, until it loses itself in the final dissolution of Pisces.

Now you can see that the zodiac is indeed a circle. The cycle of emergence, development and dissolution goes on and on, with each new generation made from what went before. Now you can see, too, why Pisces has to include everything: it is so that the following Aries stage can have the widest range of possibilities to choose from before one of them becomes a reality.

Being a Pisces isn't easy. The people of each sign represent their phase of the zodiacal cycle in society: the Arians are the initiators, the Capricorns are the achievers, and so on. How do you represent the dissolution of all forms and structures, the universal state of everything-and-nothing, when you are trying to be a normal human being?

To begin with, you are not going to be interested in physical things and their acquisition. Their most attractive features, solidity and permanence, are irrelevant to the Piscean mind, which deals with the possible rather than the real and practical. Similarly, since you are the final sign of the zodiac, you will not be trying to start anything or make something new from a situation. Nor will you be communicating anything new: as the final sign, you must be collecting the responses, not asking the questions for a later sign to answer. That eliminates Earth, Fire and Air, then; thankfully, Pisces is a Water sign. It is also Mutable; therefore it doesn't try to define anything, nor to strengthen it and keep going. So what does Pisces actually do?

It absorbs. Pisces is the most inward-looking of the signs and will receive, absorb, and use, any energy at all, and you will be quite unable to prevent yourself from doing it. You are sensitive to absolutely anything—to things which other people ignore completely. The atmosphere generated by the furnishings in a room is quite a powerful force, by your standards. So are the emotions and intentions of other people, as are the colours they wear, or the weather today. Like a photographic plate, a Piscean will faithfully absorb and represent anything he is exposed to, and he will then come to resemble that thing so closely that he is indistinguishable from the original.

This raises two important issues at once, and they will probably be familiar to you already. The first is that because you have the ability to absorb and reflect anything at all, you can be everything to everybody. This means that you can be commercially-minded in the company of stockbrokers and physically creative in the company of sculptors, yet still be sympathetic and caring in the company of demanding children. In doing all of these things you can forget who you are, and lose your individuality, which is sometimes a problem. At the same time, you can become so much a part of the scene that you are invisible; this may be what you are trying to do, and it brings us on to the second issue.

It is this: if you are so sensitive that you absorb the energies of anything you are exposed to, whether you want it or not, how do you stop yourself from coming into contact with something which you know will be damaging to you? The answer, which you probably use, even if you haven't realized what you are doing, is to remove yourself from the scene. You can do this in two ways: either by becoming invisible, which you do when you want to stay somewhere for a long time without it affecting you too much (an example of this is the way you behave at work), or by literally running away. Pisceans have a reputation for running away, which is looked on as a bad thing. It shouldn't be: after all, how else do fish defend themselves? You don't have the strength of the Fire signs or the endurance of the Earth signs, and you don't have the hard shells of your Water-sign colleagues the Cancerian crabs or the Scorpio scorpions, so when threatened you must simply make yourself scarce. As a further demonstration of that idea, consider this: each sign of the zodiac looks after a certain part of the body, and the natives of that sign tend to behave in the manner of that organ or limb. In the case of Pisces, it is the feet. What are feet for? Running!

There are some advantages of being a Pisces, though. The ones that everybody envies most are your imagination and your artistic taste. You are almost endlessly creative with your imagination—you can apparently make something out of nothing. The outside world is hungry for stories and entertainment; everybody loves fantasy and make-believe, but very few people have the imagination to create such worlds for themselves. You can. You can work with colours and music, too. A Libran has perfect taste, and a Taurean has the finest appreciation of materials, but neither of them can make an object produce an emotion in the onlooker the way you can. You have a talent for bringing people's emotions out of them, for catching a mood; only you can do this.

The reason that you are so good in these areas is to do with the fact that Pisces is the last of the signs, and represents energy at its finest and most tenuous. Most people don't realize it, but the reason that they like, say, a picture, is not because of the workmanship, or even what it represents, but because of the feelings it evokes in them. You realize this, because to you, their emotional response is more important than the picture. You are actually better at seeing what people feel about things than you are at seeing the things themselves. As soon as you meet anybody, you may not know much about them, but you know what they are feeling; you can pick up and read their emotional state. In fact, you can't *not* do it.

What do you do with all the sensations and feelings that you pick up? Most people shove them into a mental cupboard for a later date, and sort them out when they dream. Dreaming is a very useful process which we don't use half as much as we could; it gives us an opportunity to play with the meaning of things without their physical presence getting in the way, and it enables us to connect things at different levels. If that sounds like a Piscean process, it is: you have probably read somewhere before that Pisceans are supposed to be 'dreamy', and it's not a bad description. Piscean thought, the associative processes we noticed earlier, is very close to dreaming; you can combine the meanings of things in your mind, and live in a world where everything is symbolically true, but not necessarily physically true.

This is where your fantastic imagination comes from. What you are able to do, which the rest of us can't, is make a world in your imagination from your impressions of the outside world, and then live in it as though it were real. You can change it at will, and because you know that none of it is real, you don't get too upset by any of it. What you are doing, in fact, is watching movies on the inside of your head. The rest of us occasionally find you vague and preoccupied, but then we can't know what set of emotions you are enjoying at that instant; it's like trying to have a conversation with somebody who's listening to a Walkman.

You are imaginative, sensitive, and caring, but it may not be at all clear to you where you are supposed to be going. To some of you, it may not matter; if everything is in your imagination, and you don't like what you're feeling now, you know that you only have to wait for a few minutes and another experience will be along; perhaps that one will be more enjoyable. You are so *passive*, you see; you wait to be moved by the circumstance rather than make active moves yourself. The purpose of your existence, though, is to move round the zodiac, and that means towards Aries: somehow you have to define yourself, separate from all the roles that you play.

Thinking about the fishes of the sign is a very useful exercise. The water that they live in is the same as the sea of emotions and feelings that you live in. The water passes through them, and gives them life, and they cannot live without it. The currents of the water sweep them along, though they can swim against it too, if they try. You are exactly the same. It is worth noting that the sign of Pisces has two fishes, joined by a cord, but swimming in opposite directions; society pulls one way, you pull the other. The more definitely individual you are, the more you lean towards Aries. The more you allow yourself to be influenced by the crowd, the more you lean towards Aquarius. Pisces is somewhere in the middle.

Early, Middle or Late? The Decanates

Each of the zodiac signs is divided into degrees, like an arc of any other circle. Since a circle has 360 degrees, then each sign must be 30 degrees, since there are twelve signs. Each of the signs is further split into sections of ten degrees, called decanates. There are three decanates in each sign, and the one that your birthday falls in will tell you a little more about how that Piscean energy actually works in you as an individual.

First decanate (20 February–1 March)
This is the purest form of Pisces. There is a double helping of Jupiter's energy here, and that means you are even more

imaginative, even more flexible and impressionable than the other Pisceans. Early Pisceans often find that they have a hard life, full of obstacles and restrictions. It isn't really so, or no more so than anyone else's life, but when your planetary energy wants to be as mobile and as flexible as yours does, then every little obstacle seems like a major stumbling-block. In the same way, as a Mutable Water sign, you find it difficult to muster any sort of force at any one time and place; this means that you don't have the firmness of purpose to push aside things which get in your way. If your planetary energies were like a hammer, you could smash anything which obstructed you; since your energies are like running water, you have to find a way round things in your path, and you find it a bothersome business.

Early Pisceans are supposed to make good spies, and to be attracted to that kind of lifestyle. It probably has something to do with the business of being 'invisible' that we noticed earlier, as well as the fact that spies are present in all levels of society but are hidden from view. The idea of being everywhere at once but not openly so is a very Piscean one.

Second decanate (2–11 March)
Here the energy of Jupiter is mixed with that of the Moon. Bringing the Moon into the picture as well as a Mutable Water sign must surely make you think of the sea and the tides, and it is true that the sea and all that is associated with it is usually connected to this part of the sign. There are lots of Piscean sailors, but even if you have never been near the sea, you will probably find that you like going on voyages or journeys. Is it the idea of being on the move (Mutable Water)? Is it the idea of seeing new scenery and being open to new experiences (Jupiter's lunar sign)? Or is it just that you feel that there are times in life for sitting still, and times for moving on? Rhythms of time are a lunar thing, too.

The Moon also represents the general public in astrology, and your face as it is seen in public, too. If you think of how a Piscean can absorb the personality of someone else, and think of the public seeing the adopted personality instead of the real one, you can see why many Pisceans from this part of the sign want to become actors.

Finally, because moonlight is only a reflection of sunlight, a changed and paler version of the original, and in the same way that an actor's role is not the real person, this part of the sign is associated with deception and illusion. It doesn't matter whether you are the victim or the perpetrator; somehow they are part of your experience of life.

Third decanate (12–20 March)
Here Mars' strength and power are blended with Jupiter's optimistic imagination. The cocktail is an odd one, and it produces Pisceans with much more determination than the earlier decanates. Not that their energy and endurance is directed into making themselves famous, however; the direction of their interest, as always, lies inwards, and this end of the sign often finds itself attracted to areas of life where withdrawal from the world is a major feature. All forms of nursing, especially the care of the chronically sick or the incurable, are here, as are all forms of institutional work.

Although it is less common now, the idea of dedication to religion is one associated with the later stages of Pisces. There are two ways of doing this, both Piscean: the first is the hard and self-denying life of monastic orders, and the second involves the isolation, and the long voyaging, of being a missionary. You will see that there are a lot of Piscean ideas in both of those alternatives. If you were born with the Sun in this decanate, you will surely recognize the need to lose yourself in something which benefits others.

Here, too, at the very end of the zodiac, are the mysteries of life itself, and of the soul. Late Pisceans feel somehow at home in this sort of territory, and often develop their interest in it.

One unusual profession has associations with the end of Pisces: prostitution. Is it an 'invisible' service for others? Is it simply a mixture of Jupiter and Mars, or is it more than that? Late Pisceans will understand.

Three Phases of Life: Pisces as Child, Adult, Parent

The Pisces Child

Piscean children are quite sweet. That sounds like a generalization, and it is; but it is also the impression that they give, and as with everything Piscean, the impression is the most important thing. They have the ability to be whatever anybody wants them to be, and learn at an early age to alter their behaviour to suit the parent they are with at the time. Only when they have to play multiple roles at the same time do they get confused, just like the famous example of the chameleon unable to cope with being placed on a tartan rug. Whenever an argument looms, Piscean children are nowhere to be found; they can sense the change of mood, and they know that they are better off out of it altogether.

Piscean sensitivity makes for a creative and artistic child, and one who will be very successful in his early years at school. Partly this is because of his ability to be what his teacher wants him to be; the rest of it is because early schooling tries to encourage imaginative expression, and Pisceans have a better developed imagination than anybody else in the zodiac. In contrast, secondary school is often a depressing place for the young Piscean. Here there are things to be learned in a structured and organized fashion, and some subjects which are compulsory study; the changeable mind of the Piscean sees the whole organization as impossibly restricting and obstructive. He will daydream through the subjects he dislikes, turning his mind inwards to escape into a world of imagination. Being reprimanded for this leads to a further impulse to escape; a vicious circle can easily be created. Young Pisceans need a focus for their imagination, through which they can realize some sense of their own capabilities; if this is not available, they can find themselves 'being led' by the influence of others, who may not have their best interests at heart.

The Pisces Adult

Adult Pisceans spend a lot of their time avoiding pressure. You know how sensitive you are, and you also know, by the time you reach adulthood, that the rest of the world is insensitive and brutal in comparison. Like the fishes of the sign, you are sensitive to changes of pressure in the water, and try to maintain your equilibrium at all times. Situations without an obvious way out are noted and avoided, and when suddenly plunged into unfamiliar surroundings, you will always look for the door.

You have to have a constant supply of emotional experience, just as fish need water. It doesn't have to be the emotional experience of a personal relationship; anything and everything will cause you to change the way that you feel. When you can, therefore, you try to do things which make you feel good. To some extent, so does everybody else, but in your case it is the internal response which is more important than the object which produces it. Therefore you tend to like anything which can be appreciated on more than one level; you prefer poetry to prose, and you prefer paintings to maps. In each case, the emotions produced are slightly different each time you experience the poem or the painting, and you like that. You also like being able to evoke a mood or a sentiment from an old photograph, or a favourite song; you like making associations in your memory.

Associative thought isn't logical or analytical. It's personal, individual, never the same twice. It drives other people to distraction because they can't follow it, and they tend to think of you as changeable and indecisive as a result. What they can't see is that associative thought is the whole business of life for you: the most important thing about you is your imagination, and the reality that it makes for you from collecting your emotional impressions is the one that matters for you. To the other eleven signs, it's like living in a kaleidoscope; to you, it's normal.

The Pisces Parent

The difficult thing about being a Piscean parent is that it is impossible for you to be constant or firm. Whichever face you present to your child, or whichever way you try to direct them, you are likely to change your mind before long, and this can be confusing to him. The good side of this is that he is sure to have a varied upbringing, and one which offers him a much broader range of experiences than other children of his age, but the bad side is of course that he will have difficulty in seeing his parents as constant and reliable. When you need to assert your authority you will find it difficult not to sympathize with his point of view: you are sensitive enough to your child's emotional state for it to become your own, and then you will *both* be in tears.

The good thing about being a Piscean parent is that you are always receptive to what your children are trying to tell you, so that you understand intuitively what they really mean, even if their words don't carry their meaning. This works at both ends of the age range: not only can you understand a toddler who lacks the vocabulary (but not the mentality) for complex expressions, but you can also understand a teenager, whose abrasive slang hides his real emotional state.

Most Piscean parents are artistic to some extent, and a home which already contains musical instruments and artist's materials does a lot to encourage any similar talent in their children, whether or not they are Piscean. What Piscean parents *don't* have, of course, is any sort of structure in their lives; as far as they can, they will have removed all restrictions or obstacles. Some children, especially from the Earth signs, actually need an organized life; it will be up to their Piscean parents to provide it. They will find it a very difficult thing to do.

4. Pisces Relationships

How Zodiacal Relationships Work

You might think that relationships between two people, described in terms of their zodiac signs, might come in 144 varieties; that is, twelve possible partners for each of the twelve signs. The whole business is a lot simpler than that. There are only seven varieties of relationship, although each of those has two people in it, of course, and the role you play depends on which end of the relationship you are at.

You may well have read before about how you are supposed to be suited to one particular sign or another. The truth is usually different. Pisceans are supposed to get on with Cancerians and Scorpios, and indeed they do, for the most part, but it is no use reading that if you have always found yourself attracted to Libra, is it? There has to be a reason why you keep finding Librans attractive, and it is not always to do with your Sun sign; other factors in your horoscope will have a lot to do with it. The reason you prefer people of certain signs as friends or partners is because the relationship of your sign to theirs produces the sort of qualities you are looking for, the sort of behaviour you find satisfactory. When you have identified which of the seven types of basic relationship it is, you can see which signs will produce that along with your own, and then read the motivation behind it explained later on in more detail in

'The Piscean Approach to Relationships' and the individual compatibility sections.

Look at the diagram on page 16. All you have to do is see how far away from you round the zodiacal circle your partner's Sun sign is. If they are Leo, they are five signs in front of you. You are also, of course, five signs behind them, which is also important, as you will see in a little while. If they are Sagittarius, they are three signs behind you, and you are three signs in front of them. There are seven possibilities: you can be anything up to six signs apart, or you can both be of the same sign.

Here are the patterns of behaviour for the seven relationship types.

Same sign

Somebody who is of the same sign as you acts in the same way that you do, and is trying to achieve the same result for himself. If your goals permit two winners, this is fine, but if only one of you can be on top, you will argue. No matter how temperamental, stubborn, devious, or critical you can be, they can be just the same, and it may not be possible for you to take the same kind of punishment you hand out to others. In addition, they will display every quality which really annoys you about yourself, so that you are constantly reminded of it in yourself as well as in them. Essentially, you are fighting for the same space, and the amount of tolerance you have is the determining factor in the survival of this relationship.

One sign apart

Someone one sign forward from you acts as an environment for you to grow in. In time, you will take on those qualities yourself. When you have new ideas, they can often provide the encourage-ment to put them into practice, and seem to have all your requirements easily available. Often, it is this feeling that they already know all the pitfalls that you are struggling over which can be annoying; they always seem to be one step ahead of you, and can seemingly do without effort all the things which you have to sweat to achieve. If the relationship works well, they are helpful to you, but there can be bitterness and jealousy if it doesn't.

Someone one sign back from you can act as a retreat from the pressures of the world. They seem to understand your particular needs for rest and recovery, whatever they may be, and can usually provide them. They can hold and understand your innermost secrets and fears; indeed, their mind works best with the things you fear most, and the fact that they can handle these so easily is a great help to you. If the relationship is going through a bad patch, their role as controller of your fears gets worrying, and you will feel unnerved in their presence, as though they were in control of you. When things are good, you feel secure with them behind you.

Two signs apart
Someone two signs forward from you acts like a brother or sister. They are great friends, and you feel equals in each other's company; there is no hint of the parent-child or master-servant relationship. They encourage you to talk, even if you are reticent in most other company; the most frequently heard description of these relationships is 'We make each other laugh'. Such a partner can always help you put into words the things that you want to say, and is there to help you say them. This is the relationship that teenagers enjoy with their 'best friend'. There is love, but it does not usually take sexual form, because both partners know that it would spoil the relationship by adding an element of unnecessary depth and weight.

Someone two signs behind you is a good friend and companion, but not as intimate as somebody two signs forward. They are the sort of people you love to meet socially; they are reliable and honest, but not so close that things become suffocatingly intense. They stop you getting too serious about life, and turn your thoughts outwards instead of inwards, involving you with other people. They stop you from being too selfish, and help you give the best of yourself to others. This relationship, then, has a cool and a warm end; the leading sign feels much closer to his partner than the trailing sign does, but they are both satisfied by the relationship. They particularly value its chatty quality, the fact that it works even better when in a group, and its tone of affection and endearment rather than passion and obsession.

Three signs apart
Someone three signs in front of you represents a challenge of some kind or another. The energies of the pair of you can never run parallel, and so must meet at some time or another. Not head on, but across each other, and out of this you can both make something strong and well established which will serve the two of you as a firm base for the future. You will be surprised to find how fiercely this person will fight on your behalf, or for your protection; you may not think you need it, and you will be surprised that anybody would think of doing it, but it is so nonetheless.

Someone three signs behind you is also a challenge, and for the same reasons as stated above; from this end of the relationship, though, they will help you achieve the very best you are capable of in a material sense. They will see to it that you receive all the credit that is due to you for your efforts, and that everyone thinks well of you. Your reputation is their business, and they will do things with it that you could never manage yourself. It's like having your own P.R. team. This relationship works hard, gets results, and makes sure the world knows it. It also looks after itself, but it needs a lot of effort putting in.

Four signs apart
Someone four signs forward from you is the expression of yourself. All the things you wanted to be, however daring, witty, sexy, or whatever, they already are, and you can watch them doing it. They can also help you to be these things. They do things which you think are risky, and seem to get away with them. There are things you aim towards, sometimes a way of life that you would like to have, which these people seem to be able to live all the time; it doesn't seem to worry them that things might go wrong. There are lots of things in their life which frighten you, which you would lie awake at nights worrying

about, which they accept with a child's trust, and which never go wrong for them. You wish you could be like that.

Someone four signs behind you is an inspiration to you. All the things you wish you knew, they know already. They seem so wise and experienced, and you feel such an amateur; luckily, they are kind and caring teachers. They are convincing, too. When they speak, you listen and believe. It's nice to know there's somebody there with all the answers. This extraordinary relationship often functions as a mutual admiration society, with each end wishing it could be more like the other; unfortunately, it is far less productive than the three-sign separation, and much of its promise remains unfulfilled. Laziness is one of the inherent qualities of a four-sign separation; all its energies are fulfilled, and it rarely looks outside itself for something to act upon. Perhaps this is just as well for the rest of us.

Five signs apart
Someone five signs ahead of you is your technique. You know what you want to do; this person knows how to do it. He can find ways and means for you to do what you want to be involved in, and he can watch you while you learn and correct your mistakes. They know the right way to go about things, and have the clarity of thought and analytical approach necessary if you are to get things clear in your mind before you get started

Someone five signs behind you is your resource. Whenever you run out of impetus or energy, they step forward and support you. When you're broke, they lend you money, and seldom want it returned. When you need a steadying hand because you think you've over-reached yourself, they provide it. All this they do because they know that it's in their best interest as well as yours, to help you do things, and to provide the material for you to work with. You can always rely on them for help, and it's nice to know they will always be there. They cannot use all their talent on their own; they need you to show them how it should be done. Between you, you will use all that you both have to offer effectively and fully, but it is a relationship of cooperation and giving; not all the zodiac signs can make it work well enough.

Six signs apart

Someone six signs apart from you, either forwards or backwards, is both opponent and partner at the same time. You are both essentially concerned with the same area of life, and have the same priorities. Yet you both approach your common interests from opposite directions, and hope to use it in opposite ways. Where one is private, the other is public, and where one is self-centred, the other shares himself cheerfully. The failings in your own make-up are complemented by the strengths in the other; it is as if, between you, you make one whole person with a complete set of talents and capabilities. The problem with this partnership is that your complementary talents focus the pair of you on a single area of life, and this makes for not only a narrow outlook, but also a lack of flexibility in your response to changes. If the two of you are seeing everything in terms of career, or property, or personal freedom, or whatever, then you will have no way to deal effectively with a situation which cannot be dealt with in those terms. Life becomes like a seesaw; it alternates which end it has up or down, and can sometimes stay in balance; but it cannot swing round to face another way, and it is fixed to the ground so that it does not move.

These are the only combinations available, and all partnerships between two people can be described as a version of one of the seven types. It must be remembered, though, that some of the roles engendered by these dispositions of sign to sign are almost impossible to fulfil for some of the signs, because their essential energies, and the directions they are forced to take by the planets behind them, drive them in ways which make it too difficult. To form a relationship based on sharing and acceptance is one thing: to do it when you are governed by a planet like Mars is somethings else. Even when the relationship can form, the sort of approach produced by, say, Jupiter, is a very different thing from that produced by Venus.

The next thing you must consider, then, is how you, as a Pisces, attempt relationships as a whole, and what you try to find in them. Then you must lay the qualities and outlook of each of the twelve signs over the roles they must play in the seven relationship types, and see whether the pair of you manage to make the best of that relationship, or not.

The seven relationship types are common to all the signs, relating to all the other signs. You can use your understanding of them to analyse and understand the relationship between any pair of people that you know, whether or not they are Piscean; but to see how the characters fit into the framework in more detail, you will need to look at the individual compatibilities, of which just the Pisces ones are given in this book.

The Piscean Approach to Relationships

Everybody goes into a relationship for a different reason. Not everybody wants to give their all to a partner—quite a number want to get something out of the partnership without necessarily putting anything in. Pisceans aren't quite as obviously selfish as that, but it is as well to remember that Pisces is a collecting sign, and so the direction of the energies must be inwards rather than outwards.

There are two things a Pisces wants out of any relationship. The first is to generate an emotional response in himself, and on as many different levels as possible. The best kind of emotional response is that which is produced by absorbing the emotions of another person; therefore you, as a Piscean, are likely to be attracted to anybody with a strong personality, because they are emotionally 'louder', if you like, and that gives you more for your money. It doesn't really matter whether you really like your partner or not; the energy of friction and argument is just as strong, and it is the intensity of the experience that you are really after.

Another kind of emotional response is produced by being in dramatic surroundings, and you enjoy that too. Taken together, it would seem that the person who gives you most of what you want is somebody who is dramatically different, and has a lifestyle to match. This is probably the explanation for the marked tendency of Pisceans to fall for flamboyant extroverts who trample all over them.

You will have noticed that the concept of true relationship, as in friendship, rapport, and words like that, has not yet made an appearance. It isn't likely to: you're not interested in that sort of thing. If you were genuinely dependent on one other person for your emotional well-being, you would feel trapped, and would have to escape. The essential thing with a Piscean is that the experience has to keep changing—either by keeping a relationship fluid or by having a number of relationships with very different people.

You are quite capable of becoming somebody else just for the experience of it. If your partner is madly keen on sailing, you will become a weekend sailor. You will absorb his enthusiasm; you will, in fact, personify it. You will know more about sailing, in a shorter time, than you ever thought possible; you will feel perfectly at home wearing sailing clothes, whereas other people feel faintly ridiculous. Please note that none of this is permanent: what you are doing is immersing yourself in the experience of having a relationship with somebody whose passion is sailing. When, or if, the relationship comes to an end, you will step out of the role in the same way that an actor takes off his costume; and if your next intimate friend happens to be a point-to-point fanatic, you will be standing in muddy fields as though you were born to it. There is no limit to the number of times that you are prepared to perform this exercise, as long as each experience is intense enough, and different enough from the last one. You never see anything as permanent, and never hope to keep anything forever; you see people in exactly the same way. All you ask of them is that they can be intense enough to provide you with a strong emotional experience—and give you room to slip away if things look as though they are getting out of hand.

The second reason that Pisceans go into relationships of any kind is that of service to others. This quality of self-denial, the ability to lose yourself in the process of doing something on somebody else's behalf, is never far below the surface of your intentions. In relationships, it shows as the desire to befriend people who need a lot of your time and effort. These people may be ill, or unable to do things for themselves. They may be emotionally incapacitated or may have damaged themselves in some way, for instance through drink or drugs; or they may simply be demanding, selfish, and egotistical, and make large claims on your patience and time. Whatever it is, you are always ready to befriend these people. Perhaps it is because their presence draws attention away from you. It is more likely that the emotion generated by these extraordinary people is something you find interesting for its own sake. You would far rather experience anything than experience nothing.

The practicalities of a relationship are very easy for a Piscean. People find you friendly and easy to get on with; friendships form at once. There are good reasons for this, of course; what you have done is reflected back to them the friendship that they have shown you and that you have absorbed. Most people like nothing better than to be treated in the way that they would like to treat others, so the system works very well. You also know that this sort of routine generates happy emotions, and you can absorb them, too; they make you feel good.

When you fall in love, it is a full-colour experience, with stereophonic sound. What happens is that a particular person produces a response in you which you find so breathtaking that you want more of it. You know how much enjoyment you can get from your surroundings, so you alter your surroundings to produce the effects you want. By this time the affair is being conducted on the grand scale—red roses, weekends in Paris, candelit dinners, the whole thing. As each new element is added, you get more of an emotional boost from it, until you get quite delirious from the passion of it all. By this time you are a long way from reality, but that doesn't matter—what you want is the intensity of the experience, and that's what you get.

Pisceans need variety, and they need room to move. For these reasons, marriage isn't always the success you hope it might be. That doesn't mean that all Pisceans are hopeless marriage partners by any means, but you want the imaginative fantasy to continue, and sheer familiarity often brings that to an end. As long as there is interest and variety, with new experiences and new people coming and going, then you are happy; you have your current of fresh water. Whenever dull routine and predictable practicality start to predominate in a relationship, then Pisces feels that it is time to slip away and find something new and stimulating.

Individual Compatibilities Sign by Sign

All relationships between the signs work in the ways described earlier in 'How Zodiacal Relationships Work' (p.37). In addition to that, descriptions of how a Piscean attempts to form a relationship with someone from each of the twelve signs are given below. I have tried to show not what a Taurean, for example, is like, but what a Piscean sees him as, and how he sees you. Each individual Taurean looks different, of course, but their motivation is the same, and these descriptions are meant to help you understand what you are trying to do with them, and how they are trying to handle you. As usual, the words he and him can be taken to mean she and her, since astrology makes no distinctions in sex here.

Pisces-Aries

This is one of the most difficult relationships for you to form, although it is probably a little easier for you than it is for the Arian. It represents, in many ways, the unattainable ideal as far as you are concerned, in that all the things that you would like to be, the Arian already is. By being close to him you can have a taste of what it's like to be further round the zodiac than you are.

Aries is definite. He may not be much else, but he is certainly definite. He knows where he is going, and he knows how he is going to do things; what's more, he actually goes out and does them, without wasting any more time in thinking about them. His whole existence is centred around effective action; he is useless unless he is actually doing something, and he knows it. Consequently he keeps himself as busy as he possibly can, and that way he stays happy.

Being in action the whole time means that he is seldom at rest, and that he never has time to think. What's more, he never has time to consider the subtle qualities of things, and for that reason a lot of what you have to offer is lost on him. He simply isn't sensitive to the meaning of things the way you are; as far as he's concerned what you see is what you get, and the physical qualities of anything are all that matter.

From your point of view, he is everything you find appealing, and everything you are trying to avoid, all in the same package. He is simple and straightforward in his approach to life, so much so that he seems naïve at times. His physical strength and power are enormous, and yet you know that he wouldn't use them against you on purpose, because he has no malice in him. He is incapable of being devious or cruel, and you feel safe in his company. His emotions may be strong, but they are easy for you to read, and he isn't trying to trap you. You are reassured by that thought.

One of the unexpected ways in which you suit each other is that you don't crowd each other's space. When an Arian has something to do, he concentrates on doing it, which means that he ignores other people. If the truth be told, he likes his own company best, because he doesn't like wasting time talking to people when he could be active. If you are in the way when he is busy, you will sense it, and melt away in the usual Piscean fashion. He won't mind in the least; in fact he will rather appreciate it. On those occasions when you want to slip off and do something without him, he can usually find something else to do, and he won't be bothered. You can see that your preference for mobility and his preference for getting on with the job are quite compatible, though not in the way that you would immediately think.

He sees you as something almost akin to a fairy creature, a wonderful and fascinating being who vanishes when he tries to pin it down. He never understands the range of your imagination, or your emotional sensitivity, but he remains endlessly fascinated by it. He can see that you have none of his physical capabilities, and that you simply can't meet a problem head on and deal with it, and he feels that he ought to do this sort of thing for you. It is a very good arrangement, though you will have to do something in return.

What you will have to do will become apparent quite early on in the friendship. Arians have no sense of time; to them, everything happens in an eternal present. Consequently, on the odd occasions when they fail at something, they are terribly upset; like toddlers, they cannot imagine how they fell over, and how the pavement bit their knee, and how they are ever going to recover. Your job is to comfort them, and it is something you are very good at, especially as they only need it for a few minutes; you can melt away again afterwards.

You won't be able to complain about the intensity of the experience if you become lovers. Arians are all strength and drive, and you will love it—provided that you can respond strongly enough in return.

You could succeed in business together, but probably only in the media, where your imagination would be useful. He has enough drive for both of you, but he needs directing over the long term, and you may not have the firmness of purpose for that.

As marriage partners, you could make a lot of progress in the early years, but after that it looks less promising. You would eventually find him too simple and straightforward, unless he could adapt to your way of thinking.

Pisces-Taurus

This is a very easy relationship to form, and a most relaxing one to be in, for both of you. It moves extremely slowly, though, and there are no sudden moves. A friendship between you would have rhythms which would be noticeable over years, not weeks, so if you want something snappy and rapidly-changing, this isn't it.

What you will notice first about a Taurean is how steady they are. They are always going to do things their way, and in their own time, and they don't let anything put them off. This can be very reassuring. It can also be very exasperating, because when you lose your temper with them, you are not going to have the slightest effect. You could beat your tiny fists on their chest with rage all day, and they wouldn't take any notice. This is Fixed Earth, remember, and Mutable Water just runs off it like the rain from the hills. Yes, I admit that the rain eventually erodes the hills, but it does take several lifetimes.

What you have in common with a Taurean is an appreciation of the emotional qualities of material. This sounds impenetrable, I know, but there are some things which make you feel good just to be with them. Some houses are like this, and some rooms. Favourite old pullovers are like this, and so is a bowl of soup on a cold day. Pisceans appreciate the mood that these things generate, and feel reassured by it, while Taureans get to the same result from the opposite direction: they have an appreciation for the substances in themselves, and feel reassured by their warmth, familiarity, and 'rightness'.

You will realize at once that there are a lot of things you could do together which you can both enjoy in your own ways. You would probably enjoy going to the opera, for instance: the Taurean enjoys the lavish sets, the sumptuous surroundings, and the familiarity of a plot that he already knows, while you enjoy the fantasy and the drama of it all. Staying at home and entertaining is another example. Taureans are famous cooks; they have an almost magical affinity with food. From your point of view, there are the evocative smells of the kitchen, the almost invisible feeling of satisfaction radiating from a Taurean as he does the cooking, the chatter of everybody at table, and all sorts of things like that. Both of you can enjoy the atmosphere of an event, and that forms a strong bond between you.

The problems arise when the Taurean refuses to change or try anything new. No matter how much you enjoy something, you get bored with it after a while, and you long for something else. Taureans simply don't; what's more, they won't change under any circumstances. The way out, of course, is just that: it is time for you to slip away as you always do. Unfortunately, Taureans are very possessive, and they will be forced to act rather than lose you. When this happens, the outcome is very upsetting for everybody concerned.

You appreciate their stability, reliability, and appreciation of your sensitivity. They appreciate your softness and imagination, your recognition of the importance of the emotional side of things, and, though it sounds rather harsh, the fact that you are no threat to their security.

If you like your quiet life together, it can go on for years, with the friendship slipping easily into marriage. You stop them getting too dull, by providing variety; they stop you from floating away, by providing an anchor. This can be very useful if the two of you are business partners, and is of course a sure recipe for a stable marriage. Only as lovers will your differences show. He will appreciate your sense of romance, but you are likely to be bowled over by the strength of his passion. Taureans have deep and powerful passions—they just take a while to get going.

Pisces-Gemini

This one probably isn't such a good idea. It is like a knife in the water: it glitters and flashes with a wicked attractiveness, but it is sharp and deceptive to touch.

Gemini is Mutable, like you are, and his greatest assets, like yours, are his mind and his imagination; however, any similarities end there.

A Gemini analyses his surroundings, in a way that you do not. To him, every new thing is a puzzle, something that he can apply his mind to and solve. He takes situations and people apart, probing here and there, seeing what there is to see, looking at them from all possible angles; he *examines* them. When he has understood something, he plays with it if he can, to see if it does anything different, or interesting, if approached in another way.

To you this process seems horribly clinical. He seems to lose completely the essence of the experience by dissecting it. You don't work like that; you let the experience wash over you, feeling its qualities as you absorb them.

The major difference in your approach is that you are quite willing to be changed by the experience, and even to become part of it, while he is determined that he will not be affected by it in any way. He is trying to understand things from an intellectual viewpoint, and as far as possible to leave emotional responses out of it. Geminis don't have the same facility with their emotions that you do, and they tend not to enjoy them.

Because he stands apart from the things he deals with, and doesn't feel personally involved in the way that you do, he can be rather cruel; anything is reasonable, according to him, if it helps him understand what is going on. The result of this is a curiously amoral viewpoint, which shows itself from time to time in his actions and, more frequently, in what he says.

Geminis have a lot to say for themselves. They are the great talkers of the zodiac; everything they experience is converted into words and re-broadcast, in a similar process to the way you convert everything you experience into images which are stored inside your dream-memory for creative re-cycling later. The only difference between you is that the products of his experience are put out again for public consumption, whereas yours are kept for internal use only.

If you remember the similarities between what the Gemini does and what you do, then you will be able to handle him very well; you may even be able to enjoy a lot of what he comes up with. What you won't enjoy, though, is the way that he sometimes changes the truth of things. All he is doing is playing with the words, changing the order, or making adjustments to the story from time to time. It amuses him to do so, just as it amuses you to fetch images from your imagination and replay them when you are bored. The only difference is that his games come out as speech, and a lot of people don't realize that they are games. He attaches no emotional weight to what he says, of course, and doesn't expect anyone else to either.

A friendship between you can be very bright and bubbly on the surface; after all, if you mix Air and Water you can usually make foam. He will love analysing your imaginative ideas, and you will probably enjoy absorbing his observations. If the pair of you work together in any sort of business where communication is involved, you could do very well indeed. It probably isn't such a good idea to be your own bosses, though, because you are both too changeable.

Being lovers will have its problems. Geminis have no sense of romance, because to their way of thinking it is all sentimental nonsense; nor are they happy with the emotional demands of an intimate relationship. They are not particularly physical, either; you would be much better off staying as friends.

Marriage will be difficult. He will dismiss your impressionability as woolly-headedness, and you will come to dislike his sharp intellect. Besides, neither of you like things to be too stable for too long.

Pisces-Cancer

This is the first of the pairings within your element; here you find yourself in the company of somebody else whose view of life has the emotional side of things at the top. Cancer is Cardinal, though, and you are not; you will find to your surprise that these people are very determined to have things their way, and you will have no alternative but to do as they tell you.

It won't take you very long to feel familiar with the Cancerian point of view. They are careful, self-preserving individuals, and they make sure that any threats to their security are adequately dealt with in advance wherever possible. Cancerians work on the principle of defence rather than avoidance, though they have been known to dodge the issue at times; their attitude is certainly one that you understand, anyhow.

They are very protective of those they care for; if you are part of a Cancerian's 'inner circle' you know that they are doing everything they can to shield you from any harm from outside, and to give you any emotional reassurance you may need on the inside.

If you look at how they go about caring for their friends and family, you will be struck by something which is only visible to Pisceans and Scorpios, and which you would both dearly like to be able to do. Cancerians can generate emotional energy. Scorpios collect it, and Pisceans absorb and reflect it, but Cancerians actually generate it. Theirs is the original maternal instinct. The fact that they have an apparently endless source of inner strength is something you find quite wonderful, and you admire them very much. It seems so much better a thing to be than what you are at the moment; they seem to be able to do without effort all the things you have to work at.

It may help you to get your relationship into perspective if you consider that the two of you are separated by the scale on which you work. To be sure, the Cancerian seems to be so much more intense, to care so deeply for others—but then Cancer works on the level of a parent to a child, on an individual basis. Pisces is a much more widely-dispersed form of the same energy; Pisces can care for everybody, not just your immediate friends and relatives. What is concentrated in one place can't be everywhere at once, and vice versa.

A friendship between you will be very easily formed; you instinctively understand, and identify with, each other's likes and dislikes. Once you have got to know each other a little better, you will find that you allow yourself to be led by the Cancerian. He will do things in the way that is best for him, and you will align yourself, Mutable as always, so that you are both facing the same way. The odd thing about this is that although he is leading, he isn't leading you anywhere new or interesting, and you will get bored. Your need for security doesn't work in the same way as his—you know that you can vanish when things get tight, and he knows that he can't. Therefore you don't mind seeking out new experiences just to see what they're like, but they are sure to worry your Cancerian. You may be timid in comparison with an Arian, but against a Cancerian you are positively rash.

Being lovers is likely to be a very rewarding experience for you both. Cancerians are stronger physically than you might imagine, but their true interest lies in the emotional relationship behind the sexual one. They are as sensitive to the little details of romance as you are, but they have a stronger passion, which you will enjoy. The only trouble is that they are possessive. Not quite to the extent that Taureans are, but more than you would like them to be, all the same.

As long-terms partners, both in business and in marriage, there is the problem of restricted progress to be dealt with. He is effective, but not adventurous; you are the other way round. One of you, at least, has to have both qualities if you are to do more than merely stay your ground.

Pisces-Leo

Here you meet somebody who is different from you in every way, and yet who seems to have a great affinity with you. They don't have your love of variety, and they are completely insensitive to the feelings of others at times, and yet you can't help liking them.

The most useful way of comparing you is by looking at actors and the way they perform. It's not a bad analogy, because you both feel very much at home in the theatre, and you may well meet your Leo in a theatrical setting. If a Piscean actor works through reflection, then the Leonine one works through projection. You are well aware of the way you allow yourself to absorb and represent what people want you to be; when your audience looks at you they see in you what they want to see, and you are happy to reflect their expectations back at them. Leos don't work that way at all. They project themselves through the role they are playing, so that their own energy shines out from behind the costume. Nobody in the audience is in the slightest doubt who it is that they are watching. They know that they are seeing the actor rather than the character, but they don't mind. Leos are the stars of the show; the audience would rather see them being themselves than see them in character.

From your point of view, being close to a Leo can be a very good idea. They simply radiate warmth and fun: wherever they are is the place to be. If you can absorb this from them, and it isn't hard for somebody like you, then you can have as good a time as they do. The clever part comes in being not quite as Leonine as they are, because there is only room for one of them in their world, and they resent competition quite strongly, but you are more than sensitive enough to spot that situation in its early stages, and melt back into the background for a while.

Together you will have a very good time indeed. Everybody loves a Leo, and they have lots of friends. For somebody like you, who likes dramatic and interesting people, and plenty of variety, their social circle should provide you with more than enough emotional energy for your needs. There are odd occasions when a Leo feels unloved and unsure of himself, and he is difficult to comfort then; still, your ability to be there when you're needed and not when you're not is most likely to give the Leo what he needs.

He sees you as somebody who seems to sparkle all the more brightly as he puts more energy into you, and he likes to see that. He also sees you as an imaginative source of new ideas, which he can put into practice. He doesn't feel that he's stealing your ideas, because he knows that you probably don't have the capacity to make your dreams real in the way that he does—and he's right. It is a mutually beneficial arrangement for both of you; your imagination is tied to his ability to organize and make things happen. Without your ideas, it must be said, he would run out of things to do.

Friendship between you looks like the attraction of opposites, and on the surface it probably is. To begin with, you will play roles with each other, preferring to stay behind your masks until you get to know each other better. Even when you have been together a long time, there will be little routines that you will perform with each other for fun. At a deeper level (which the outside world does not see) you will realize that you are both very useful to each other over the long term, too, and that you probably need each other to get the best from yourselves.

As lovers, the only problem you should have is whether you can afford it all; once Leo has shown you how to turn your fantasies into extravagant realities it's difficult to stop.

As business partners, provided that the business itself isn't too dull, you will be wonderful together. Similarly, marriage is a good idea too, as long as you don't let it become all work and no play. Keep things bright and the marriage will last forever.

Pisces-Virgo
You probably expect things to be difficult with a person who represents the opposite sign to your own, and you won't be disappointed. What is likely to annoy you more than anything

else about him is his ability to pin you down and hurt you; the fact that he doesn't really mean to hurt you only makes it worse.

Virgo is Mutable, just like you are; that means that he is at least as quick on the uptake as you are, and he doesn't mind if things keep changing, either. He is an Earth sign, though, and that gives him patience and endurance in a way that your Water sign doesn't. In addition, he deals with the real world—feelings are very low on his list of priorities.

Like the Gemini, his mind is sharp and penetrating, but it has a disconcerting 'dryness' to it; emotion and sentiment aren't there at all, and you will find it difficult to come to terms with that. What he does have, though, is a talent for analysis and understanding, and it frightens you.

The overall feeling, as far as you are concerned, is one of precision. You are interested only in how your car feels, and whether a different one would make you feel any better. Virgos are interested in how their car works and whether they can do anything to make it any more efficient. In the same way, you eat the food you like, but Virgos eat the food that does them good. Whether they like it doesn't come into the argument—but if it wasn't good for them they wouldn't eat it, no matter how good it tasted.

Virgo understands everything in a very precise way. He will be able to say exactly what it is that you are doing, and why. He will also be able to tell you how to do it better. This is a very painful process for you: you are used to being able to please yourself, with nobody able to define you precisely. Your vagueness and constant mobility is both your greatest defence and your greatest pride—but Virgo can pin you down and tell you what you're doing. Speared fish tend to writhe a bit, and you are no exception. The reason the Virgo does it, though, is because he wants to help. Impossible to believe? Not if you think about it for a minute. He is Mutable, remember, as Gemini is, and as you are. His way of reacting to outside influences is to break them down and analyse them, until he understands what makes them the way they are. Then he tries to make a better world by putting things back together in a better order. In other words, he tries to improve things where he can, for everybody's benefit.

You see him as short-sighted, over-critical, and unfeeling. What you should see him as is somebody who is as familiar with the workings of material things as you are with the workings of emotion and sentiment, but whose special interest leads him to examine smaller and smaller details, while yours leads you to deal with larger and more universal feelings and ideas. His energies are focused and concentrated; you are unfocused and diffuse. You are simply at opposite ends of the zodiac, and that's all there is to it.

He sees you as disordered, vague, and something of a victim of circumstance. He can just about believe that such a person as you, completely unfamiliar with the details of the real world, could exist, but he is sure that you need his help. What he should see, but probably can't or won't, is that the world of the imagination is just as real as any other, and that being receptive to it opens up huge realms of experience which are otherwise inaccessible. His security comes from knowing what's going on; yours comes from knowing that you can run away from trouble if things get difficult. He threatens your mobility, and you threaten his understanding of the world: no wonder you feel that you are attracting each other.

Friendship will only grow if you each trust the other not to invade your own world. As lovers, you will find Virgo's range of response rather limited, while his unintentional criticisms may wound you at vulnerable moments.

As business partners, as with a marriage, you will really need a third element (a common project or another person) to help bridge the gap between the areas in which you function best.

Pisces-Libra

Although this one ought to be similar to the Leo relationship, and although it is true that it does work best on an artistic, or at least a personal, level, the fact remains that it is less satisfying in many respects than the Leo one is. Why?

The probable answer is that this relationship is too soft. Both of you are known for your affability, for your willingness to fit in with other people's wishes and preferences. The trouble is that neither of you like being the one to make the decisions, and if you are both looking for a lead from the other then you may not get anywhere at all.

You will get a better idea of what is actually happening if you look more closely at what the Libran is trying to do. He's not somebody who absorbs energy from others; that's your territory, and yours alone. What he's trying to do is to promote agreement and balance. He wants to find points of contact, and if possible points of agreement, between himself and anybody else he meets. He starts on a fairly simple level, by enthusing about the same things that you do, but it soon extends to all sorts of other areas. The point of it all, as far as he's concerned, is to link himself to you as a balanced partner, perfectly matching or counterbalancing all the quirks in your character with all of the quirks in his. The problem is that he can only do this on a one-to-one basis, but feels a need to do it with everybody he knows. What he ends up with is a series of intimate friends, all of whom are convinced that they are his special partner.

From your point of view there is a good side and a bad side to this. The good side is that he usually has a varied and active social life, so that he can build as many friendships as he can. He needs to stay in circulation; he is an Air sign, and they need to keep moving. You are a fish who likes to swim in running water, too, so the two of you will enjoy being in company as much as you enjoy being together.

The bad side is that you may feel tied by his idea of relationship. Librans aren't jealous, but relationships are the only things that really matter to them; they can't function unless they have somebody by their side. While you may be quite happy, and indeed flattered, to play that role for a while, there will come a time when you feel like slipping away for a bit. Without a partner they are lost—how can you do it? And how can you be the partner they need, who must counterbalance what they have to offer, when you can only absorb and reflect what you receive? The fact is that they need somebody firm and active to take the decisions for them, and preferably somebody with some sort of talent in the real world. Your world of moods and impressions is no place for a Libran; he can only relate to one thing at a time.

Friendship between you is best if it centres around a shared interest. He would dearly love to add your sensitivity to his own artistic tastes, while your rather uncontrolled emotional whirl could benefit from some of his balance and order. Libran order isn't restricting in any way, it simply makes things nicer and puts them into a better relationship to each other, to create more pleasant effect. You could probably do with some of that. As you can see, you have a lot that you can give to each other, and a lot that you can take. What you have to do is give and take freely, but with both of you standing up, unsupported. The moment you start to lean on one another, you'll fall over.

Should you fall in love, which is all too easy for you both, the affair may well resemble something from a Mills and Boon romance. Remember that such a relationship is a sort of ideal for a Libran, and he will enjoy the relationship far more than he enjoys the person he shares it with. You are similar; your imagination goes into overdrive when you are given a chance to surround yourself with the paraphernalia of romantic love. In a way, then, neither of you are *really* in love with the other person, which is possibly just as well.

In a long-term relationship, either in business or as a married couple, the problem of decision-making will recur. One of you has got to be realistic, and it will probably be the Libran at the end of the day; he is a Cardinal sign, after all. You could be dithering for a long time, though, while he makes up his mind.

Pisces-Scorpio

This is the sort of thing you have been promising yourself. Like a diet of chocolate cake, it will do you no good, and you know it, but you don't care a bit. Scorpio is a Water sign, like yourself, but with the kind of force and intensity you can only dream about. He will chew you up and spit you out, of course. You know that you can escape in the usual way, but you also know that he can probably find you, wherever you hide, and you're not at all sure that you want to escape anyway. Scorpio is a very dangerous drug, but if addiction is the price of ecstasy, then you're prepared to pay.

Scorpio seems to have all that you've ever wanted, in many respects. He is so sure of what he wants, for a start. When he has decided on something, he will go straight for it; it may take him a while to get it, because there will inevitably be people in the way, but he will get it in the end, and he won't take as long over it as many would have done. Like you, he is sensitive to the feelings of those around him, and he lives in a world where hopes and fears are much more important than bricks and mortar. He is not afloat or adrift in this world, though, as you are; he knows exactly where he is going, and he doesn't allow himself to be influenced by what's around him. His confidence in himself, and his sense of purpose, are much too sure for that. He is a predator in your home waters.

What you want from him is to be able to bask in the power he puts out. He is so emotionally powerful that being near him is like getting a mild electric shock—he makes you tingle. We have mentioned before that you want the intensity of the experience more than you want it to be good or bad, and you will find this person's company simply irresistible. Most people think that Scorpios are very sexy: they are, but only because sexual energy, that is the energy of Mars, is the only sort that they have to play with. What it works out as in real life is that Scorpios do everything with the intensity that other people reserve for sex only. You don't really care: it is simply the most intense energy you have ever experienced, and you want to be near the source of it.

What could he ever want from you? He has most of your sensitivity, and he is far more effective and controlled, you think: as far as you can see, you have nothing that he could possibly want. He wants two things, one on the surface and one from very deep down in your soul. Firstly, he wants to be invisible, and secondly, he wants your confidence. The first part, being invisible, is relatively easy to understand. Scorpio needs to know all that he can about everybody who is around him. and for that reason he has developed the habit of digging deeply into people's past history so that he has all the information he needs. He is rather obvious while he does so, though, or so he thinks; nobody could miss that intensity of energy when it is put to work (in fact, most people miss it completely, because they just don't have the sensitivity of the Water signs; but that doesn't stop the Scorpio from feeling obvious as he does his researches). Being able to disguise himself by fading into the background is something he would love to be able to do. He wouldn't become part of the background, as you do, he would just like it: his sense of identity and purpose would still be there. Devious, yes?

The second part, about wanting your confidence, is more difficult. It is simply that the reason that a Scorpio is so powerful and so secretive is that he is protecting himself. He doesn't trust himself, and that's the truth. You have the confidence to cast yourself upon the waters and see what comes along: he daren't do that, not ever, and he thinks that your habit of doing so is truly wondrous. Perhaps, over a very long time, you could teach him how to relax, to be trusting, and not to worry.

Having a friendship, an affair, a marriage, or going into business with a Scorpio all boil down to the same thing from your point of view. You are so helplessly drunk on his sheer magnetism that you are of almost no practical use to him anyway, but ask yourself this: do you want a relationship that leaves you as limp as a wet rag from the intensity of it all the whole time? Have you the strength for it?

Pisces-Sagittarius
This is a lot better than you would think. Not only do you have the same quality—you are both Mutable signs—but you share a planet too: Jupiter. Not many pairings work in this way; Gemini and Virgo is the only other one.

What you have in common is your optimism, your imagination, and your sense of fantasy. Both of you have the geniune ability to greet the future with enthusiasm, because you are sure that it will be interesting and worthwhile. None of the other signs can do this. Partly it comes from your belief that no serious harm will come to you, and partly because you both get bored easily, and welcome anything by way of a change or novelty.

Sagittarius isn't living in a dream world in the same way that you are. He's in the real world, making huge progress and bounding along from one adventure to the next; his humour and optimism never let him down, and he gets out of trouble time and time again by an almost uncanny blend of sheer talent and the most sublime good luck.

He has the warmth of Leo and the adventurous dash of Aries too, but he has something over and above them both: he has imagination, and he has knowledge. Sagittarius' mental capacities are the most highly developed of all of the Fire signs, and may even exceed those of Gemini. He can think logically and clearly, sure, but what characterizes his thought is that his heart is in it: in other words, he believes in what he says, and it is the emotion behind the thought that makes him so much more attractive to you than Gemini or Virgo.

He doesn't have your sensitivity, and he would rather live in the real world than your world of moods and feelings, but he knows that your world exists, and he is curious to find out more. His interest helps you warm to him; he is sure enough of his own position not to feel the need to challenge you, or frighten you away. In addition, his enthusiasm and genuine good humour are there for you to absorb and enjoy.

He doesn't cling, because he values his freedom, and assumes that you do the same. He is loyal and trustworthy, though, because he is already so secure that there is no advantage for him in being dishonest. Besides, his principles are higher than that.

You see him as a sort of labrador retriever: friendly, bouncy, and loyal, always ready for a new adventure, and sure that it will be fun. When you look at the real world, and the people in it, it always seems to you that they are having such a dull time; a Sagittarian is the only person, you think, who seems to have struck the right balance between responsibility and enjoyment, and who hasn't let the search for material security close the doors of his imagination.

He sees you as representing the finer things in life, and its subtler values, too. Whenever daily life gets too dull for him, a few minutes with you will re-awaken his imagination and let him see the meanings behind the things he does. This in turn re-awakens his intellect, his knowledge, and his wisdom. He needs you as a sort of pure source, to which from time to time he returns for refreshment.

You wouldn't want to be each other, but you like and admire each other a great deal; for this reason any friendship between you will be close and loyal. You might not want to become lovers, but if you do, you will find that his bounciness extends to all areas of his life, often at the expense of subtlety. There are better business partnerships than this one, because you would both sooner change directions than stick at something if it doesn't work at the first attempt, but it's not at all bad as a marriage. You have the humour and the imagination to see past your immediate problems to a brighter future ahead.

Pisces-Capricorn

There can be no more unlikely pairing, on the surface, than the soft and sensitive Piscean and the hard-headed, taciturn Capricorn. Yet this is a useful and satisfying pairing; it is based on alliance and help rather than power and passion, but it is none the worse for being gentle, and none the less deep either.

Capricorns are not the world's great communicators. They have a fairly fixed view of the world, and they work long hours to fulfil what they see as their duty to those both above and below them in the order of things. They are well-regulated people, who keep their feelings to themselves, for the most part, and devote any spare energy that they may have to bettering themselves.

They are not dumb, but they take a while to get talking, and they are not very expressive. You are the ideal person to listen to them: they express their feelings as strongly as they can, but it takes somebody as sensitive as you to realize that they are in fact shouting. Capricorns are very grateful for the attention that you give them, and particularly for the way that you get the message the first time, so that they don't have to go through the agony of trying to express themselves twice. They don't like being told what to do, and they don't like people who pull them away from the things that they have to get done. Luckily, you don't do either of those things. Your energies are too slight to move the Earth of a Capricorn, and anyway you don't have enough push to change the direction of a Cardinal sign. Nor do you stay when they don't want you; you know when they are busy, and you fade away.

Like elephants, they don't forget. If there's anything that you would like them to do, they will do it for you, because you have been kind enough to listen to them from time to time, and they are therefore in your debt (as they will no doubt see it). As it happens, there is a great deal that they can do for you, and they don't have to move a muscle to do it—they have only to be themselves. It is simply this: your own life can get a bit hectic from time to time, and you often allow yourself to get swept away by something that takes your fancy. It is very reassuring to have some kind of constant, something unchanging to which you can relate, and to which you can compare your experiences—a sort of anchor and yardstick in one. It is, of course, much nicer if that constant can be a person, and in the Capricorn you have exactly that.

Capricorn will enjoy listening to your experiences. They will sound very outlandish to him, and he will be very thankful that he doesn't live in your world, but he will enjoy hearing them nonetheless. You keep him up to date; the Earth doesn't feel quite so dry and dull when the flowing Water of Pisces has washed over it.

Friendship between you, then, is a quiet and fond affair, often conducted over long periods of time. Neither of you needs frequency of contact to intensify the experience: it isn't going to get any more exciting, and anyway that isn't the point here. Besides, you both have plenty of other things to do, and if the other one were around more he'd only be in the way.

As a lover, you might like his slow and traditional approach, but there again you might not. He will be constant, but that isn't always important to you; will you be faithful to him, or will you let yourself be swept away by newer and stronger passions?

A Capricorn as a business partner is always a good idea: business is his home ground. He will probably do more for you than you for him in this respect; the best thing for you to do would be to reflect his energies, and do things the way he does them.

Marriage could be a good idea—perhaps better than most people would imagine. Everything with a Capricorn gets better over the long term, and you could benefit from his steadiness, provided that he doesn't expect you to be like him all the time. He will be very successful, given time; if you'd like to share in his success in return for being his companion and confidant, then stay with him.

Pisces-Aquarius

A relationship between yourself and the sign which is behind you in the zodiacal sequence is always difficult. The people of that sign always seem to be particularly hostile to your way of thought, and yet they can be a great support to you, if you would let them be so.

Aquarians are too cool for you. They are analytical, like Virgos, but on a scale similar to your own. At least you could retreat from a Virgo's nitpicking by thinking of finer and higher things, but the Aquarian can follow you into your imagination, and shoot you down from there. You can speak to him of passion and beauty, and of Art with a capital A, and he will speak to you of the spirit of the times, the pleasing optical effect of regular and proportional shapes, and of the Expressionist movement. What to you seems achingly personal is to him highly impersonal, and can be explained and analysed away. He will not allow you to think that what you feel is in any way individual and unique; to do so, for him, would be to suggest that collective thought, where everybody shares the same opinion, is in some way not possible.

He will encourage you to think, and especially to speak, to express your thoughts, because he is an Air sign; what he doesn't hold with is the business of feeling, which to you is the most important part of expression, and more important than thinking.

Perhaps it is because they can see the meanings that lie beyond our normal actions that the Aquarian upsets you so. Only he and Sagittarius can appreciate your world, and you feel that Sagittarius is on your side because his brain and his heart work side by side; for cool Aquarians, though, the brain is definitely the senior partner. It may also be the fact that he is indeed so cool emotionally which upsets you; he will cast a very faint shadow indeed in your world of feelings, and so it will be difficult for you to see him properly.

You can get very angry with him, if you try. The thing that really makes you mad is how, for all his wide ranging interests and his willingness to get involved with political or humanitarian causes, he never really seems to get *involved*—or at least not by your standards. If he got carried away by his arguments or his beliefs, or if he cared enough for something to give his all for it—just *once*—then you'd forgive him. What you want is for his confounded know-it-all smartness to be completely submerged in the passion of the event, but you know it won't happen.

Do you know why you do this? Because you fear that you might be just like that. You have this nagging doubt in the back of your mind that you might be as cool and unmoved as he is, watching life's experiences float by you like so many video films. You're not like that, of course, you're much, much more involved; but because you are concerned to experience things as intensely as possible, to really *become* each new thing as it passes, you worry that you might not be using yourself as well as you might. That's what you don't like about Aquarians; they are what you see if you look over your own shoulder to see where you came from.

If you don't let him worry you, and you don't get angry, the two of you can have a very pleasant time. Aquarians are accomplished socializers: in fact, they are at their very best in company, more so even than the rest of the Air signs. They are bright conversationalists, too, so things need never be dull; just don't look for the personal intensity of experience that is so important to you. They're not you, remember.

It's probably not such a good idea to become lovers; they are much less successful on a one-to-one basis, and they don't have the emotional range that you find so desirable.

There are worse people to go into business with, but you won't enjoy their way of working, so why bother?

Marriage is possible, but not necessarily a good thing, unless you are both prepared to try and see things from the other's point of view. You could do each other a lot of good, but you may not choose to see it that way.

Pisces-Pisces

A partnership with somebody from your own sign emphasizes the mutual talents and shortcomings of the pair of you. In the case of two Pisceans, it is almost impossible to say which way it will turn out; you can take your pick from hundreds of roles, and can play any one of them.

Pisces, perhaps more than the other signs, works on more than one level at once. At the very least, there is an outward appearance and an inner meaning; often there are quite a number of stages in between as well, as well as a few further on and further out, if you see what I mean.

Consequently, the union between two Pisceans can take almost any form. At the very highest level, it may be an almost telepathic rapport between two musicians or dancers, who seem to know in advance what the other is about to do. It may be a long and caring friendship, where each intuitively knows what the other would or wouldn't like, without having to ask. Then again, it may be two people from widely different lives, who trust each other and enjoy getting very drunk in each other's company every Thursday night.

You won't be able to give each other encouragement but you will be able to give each other *dis*couragement, in that you will be able to suggest escape routes to each other, so that you can avoid being decisive or, even worse, definite about things.

You can have no secrets from each other; each of you is sensitive enough to be able to read the other quite easily. After a few futile exercises in one-upmanship, you should come to trust one another, simply because you have no alternative, and because you have more to offer each other by being constructive and helpful than not. Eventually you will begin to use your relationship as somewhere to offload emotional rubbish which you have picked up recently; you can have a great deal of fun sorting through each other's experiences. It's a bit like living in a scrapyard; after a while you get quite good at spotting the useable items from the junk.

You can stop each other getting lonely, in a very specialized way. Only another Piscean can appreciate things on the sort of levels of meaning that are important to you, and therefore only another Piscean can help if you want to talk about those levels of experience, or to offload them onto somebody else. The other signs can usually find somebody from elsewhere in the zodiac besides their own sign who will understand what they are trying to say, but for a Piscean only another one will do.

This isn't the sort of relationship you get into because you want it to go somewhere; this is the one you choose precisely because you know that it won't. This is the sloppy armchair of friendships: it's no good for your back, and it doesn't look very smart, but you can come home, kick off your shoes, and fall into it with a sigh. You know who your friends are.

For exactly the same reasons it makes a very poor business partnership. Neither of you is assertive enough, and to focus your energies in the commercial world you need somebody other than another Piscean.

As lovers, you are likely to encourage each other's worst habits. It will be a very private relationship, because you know that no outsider will be able to appreciate what is going on. At its highest level, it will be sublime, almost spiritual; at its lower levels, you will simply indulge each other's sloppiness.

If you choose this pairing for marriage, it is because you definitely want it to be a retreat from the world, somewhere you can stop acting for a while. Perhaps you have a strenuous public life. It's not a marriage which in itself is ambitious or progressive, but it could be just what you are looking for—the one place where you don't have to be invisible.

Part 3

Your Life

5. The Year within Each Day

You have probably wondered, in odd moments, why there are more than twelve varieties of people. You know more than twelve people who look completely different. You also know more than one person with the same Sun sign as yourself who doesn't look anything like you. You also know two people who look quite like each other, but who are not related, and do not have birthdays near each other, so can't be of the same Sun sign. You will have come to the conclusion that Sun signs and astrology don't work too well, because anyone can see that there are more than twelve sorts of people.

You will also have wondered, as you finished reading a newspaper or magazine horoscope, how those few sentences manage to apply to a twelfth of the nation, and why it is that they are sometimes very close to your true circumstances, and yet at other times miles off. You will have come to the conclusion that astrology isn't all that it might be, but some of it is, and that you like it enough to buy magazines for the horoscopes, and little books like this one.

It might be that there is some other astrological factor, or factors, which account for all the different faces that people have, the similarities between people of different Sun signs, and the apparent inconsistencies in magazine horoscopes. There are, indeed, lots of other astrological factors we could consider, but one in particular will answer most of the inconsistencies we have noticed so far.

It is the Ascendant, or rising sign. Once you know your Ascendant, your way of working, your tastes, your preferences and dislikes, and your state of health (or not, as the case may be). It is perhaps of more use to you to consider yourself as belonging to your Ascendant sign, than your Sun sign. You have been reading the wrong newspaper horoscopes for years; you are not who you thought you were!

You are about to protest that you know when your birthday is. I'm sure you do. This system is not primarily linked to your birthday, though. It is a smaller cogwheel in the clockwork of the heavens, and we must come down one level from where we have been standing to see its movements. Since astrology is basically the large patterns of the sky made small in an individual, there are a number of 'step-down' processes where the celestial machinery adjusts itself to the smaller scale of mankind; this is one of them.

Here's the theory:

Your birthday pinpoints a particular time during the year. The Sun appears to move round the strip of sky known as the zodiac during the course of the year. In reality, of course, our planet, Earth, moves round the Sun once a year, but the great friendly feature of astrology is that it always looks at things from our point of view; so, we think we stand still, and the Sun appears to move through the zodiac. On a particular day of importance, such as your birthday, you can see which of the zodiac signs the Sun is in, pinpoint how far it has gone in its annual trip round the sky, and then say 'This day is important to me, because it is my birthday; therefore this part of the sky is important to me because the Sun is there on my special day; what are the qualities of that part of the Sun's journey through the zodiac, and what are they when related to me?' The answer is what you usually get in a horoscope book describing your Sun sign.

Fine. Now let's go down one level, and get some more detail. The Earth rotates on its own axis every day. This means that, from our point of view, we stand still and the sky goes round us once a day. Perhaps you hadn't thought of it before, but that's how the Sun appears to move up and across the sky from sunrise to sunset. It's actually us who are moving, but we see it the other way round. During any day, then, your birthday included, the whole of the sky goes past you at some time or another; but at a particular moment of importance, such as the time that you were born, you can see where the Sun is, see which way up the sky is, and say, 'This moment is important to me, because I was born at this time; therefore the layout of the sky has the same qualities as I do. What are the qualities of the sky at this time of day, and what are they when related to me?'

You can see how you are asking the same questions one level lower down. The problem is that you don't know which bit of the sky is significant. Which bit do you look at? All you can see? All that you can't (it's spherical from your point of view, and has no joins; half of it is below the horizon, remember)?

How about directly overhead? A very good try; the point in the zodiac you would arrive at is indeed significant, and is used a lot by astrologers, but there is another one which is more useful still. The eastern horizon is the point used most. Why? Because it fulfils more functions than any other point. It gives a starting point which is easily measurable, and is even visible (remember, all astrology started from observations made before mathematics or telescopes). It is also the contact point between the sky and the earth, from our point of view, and thus symbolizes the relationship between the sky and mankind on the earth. Finally, it links the smaller cycle of the day to the larger one of the year, because the Sun starts its journey on the eastern horizon each day as it rises; and, if we are concerned with a special moment, such as the time of your birth, then the start of the day, or the place that it started, at any rate, is analogous to the start of your life. Remember that you live the qualities of the moment you were born for all of your life; you are that moment made animate.

The point in the zodiac, then, which was crossing the eastern horizon at the time you were born, is called the Ascendant. If this happened to be somewhere in the middle of Gemini, then you have a Gemini Ascendant, or Gemini rising, whichever phrase you prefer. You will see that this has nothing to do with the time of year that you were born, only with the time of day.

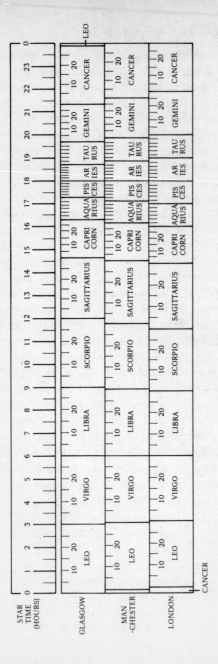

Different signs are on the horizon at different times according to where you live, as you can see. This is because of the difference in latitude. If you live in between the places given, you can make a guess from the values here. To compensate for longitude, subtract twelve minutes from your birthtime if you live in Glasgow, Liverpool or Cardiff; ten minutes for Edinburgh or Manchester, and six minutes for Leeds, Tyneside, or the West Midlands. *Add* four minutes for Norwich.

Have a look at the diagram opposite, which should help explain things. If two people are born on the same day, but at different times, then the Ascendant will be different, and the Sun and all the other planets will be occupying differentparts of the sky. It makes sense to assume, then, that they will be different in a number of ways. Their lives will be different, and they will look different. What they will have in common is the force of the Sun in the same sign, but it will show itself in different ways because of the difference in time and position in the sky.

How do you know which sign was rising over the eastern horizon when you were born? You will have to work it out. In the past, the calculation of the Ascendant has been the subject of much fuss and secrecy, which astrologers exploit to the full, claiming that only they can calculate such things. It does take some doing, it is true, but with a few short cuts and a calculator it need only take five minutes.

Here is the simplest routine ever devised for you to calculate your own Ascendant, provided that you know your time of birth. Pencil your answers alongside the stages as you go, so you know where you are.

1. Count forwards from 20 February to your birthday: 20 February is 1, 21 February is 2, and so on.
   Total days: *O* . . . .
2. Add 152 to this. New total is: *152* . . . .
3. Divide by 365, and then
4. Multiply by 24. Answer is now: . . . *9.984* . . . .
   (Your answer by now is between 0 and 24. If it isn't, you have made a mistake somewhere. Go back and try again).

5. Add your time of birth, in 24-hour clock time. If you were born at 3 p.m., that means 15. If you were born in Summer Time, take one hour off. If there are some spare minutes, your calculator would probably like them in decimals, so it's 0.1 of an hour for each six minutes. 5.36 p.m. is 17.6, for example. Try to be as close as you can. New total is: . . . .

6. If your total exceeds 24, subtract 24. Your answer must now

be between 0 and 24. Answer is: . . . .

7. You have now got the time of your birth not in clock time, but in sidereal, or star, time, which is what astrologers work in. Page 72 has a strip diagram with the signs of the zodiac arranged against a strip with the values 0 to 24, which are hours in star time. Look against the time you have just calculated, and you will see which sign was rising at the time you were born. For example, if your calculated answer is 10.456, then your Ascendant is about the 16th degree of Scorpio.

What Does the Ascendant Do?

Broadly speaking, the Ascendant does two things. Firstly, it gives you a handle on the sky, so that you know which way up it was at the time you entered the game, so to speak; this has great significance later on in the book, when we look at the way you handle large areas of activity in your life such as your career, finances, and ambitions. Secondly, it describes your body. If you see your Sun sign as your mentality and way of thinking, then your Ascendant sign is your body and your way of doing things. Think of your Sun sign as the true you, but the Ascendant as the vehicle you have to drive through life. It is the only one you have, so you can only do with it the things of which it is capable, and there may be times when you would like to do things in a different way, but it 'just isn't you'. What happens over your life is that your Sun sign energies become adapted to specifically express themselves to their best via your Ascendant sign, and you become an amalgam of the two. If you didn't, you would soon become very ill. As a Pisces with, say, a Taurean Ascendant, you do things from a Pisces motivation, but in a Taurean way, using a Taurean set of talents and abilities, and a Taurean body. The next few sections of the book explain what this means for each of the Sun/Ascendant combinations.

Some note ought to be made of the correspondence between the Ascendant and the actual condition of the body. Since the Ascendant sign represents your physical frame rather than the personality inside it, then the appearance and well-being of that frame is also determined by the Ascendant sign. In other words, if you have a Libra Ascendant, then you should look like a Libran, and you should be subject to illnesses in the parts of the body with a special affinity to that sign.

The Astrology of Illness

This is worth a book in itself, but it is quite important to say that the astrological view of illness is that the correlation between the individual and the larger universe is maintained. In other words, if you continue over a long period of time with a way of behaviour that denies the proper and necessary expression of your planetary energies, then the organ of your body which normally handles that kind of activity for your body systems will start to show the stresses to you. A simple example: Gemini looks after the lungs, which circulate air, and from which oxygen is taken all over the body. Gemini people need to circulate among a lot of people, talking and exchanging information. They act as the lungs of society, taking news and information everywhere. They need to do this to express their planetary energies, and society needs them to do this or it is not refreshed, and does not communicate. You need your lungs to do this, too. Lungs within people, Geminis within society: same job, different levels. If you keep a Gemini, or he keeps himself, through circumstance or ignorance, in a situation where he cannot talk or circulate, or where he feels that his normal status is denied, then he is likely to develop lung trouble. This need not be anything to do with a dusty atmosphere, or whether he smokes, although obviously neither of those will help; they are external irritants, and this is an internal problem caused by imbalance in the expression of the energies built into him since birth. In the sections which follow, all the observations on health are to do with how the body shows you that certain behaviour is unbalancing you and causing unnecessary stress; problems from these causes are alleviated by listening to yourself and changing your behaviour.

Your Ascendant

Aries Ascendant

If you have Aries rising, you are an uncommon individual, because Aries only rises for about fifty minutes out of the twenty-four hour day. You must have been born sometime after breakfast, or else you have got your sums wrong somewhere.

What you are trying to do with yourself is project a Pisces personality through an Arian vehicle. You will always be trying to do things faster than anybody else, and this can lead to hastiness and a certain degree of accident-proneness. What you see as the correct way to do things involves immediate action by the most direct method, to secure instant, and measurable, results. You feel that unless you are directly and personally responsible for doing things, then they cannot be done, not only because you believe that only you can do them properly, but because you get no satisfaction from letting anybody else do anything. Personal experience of everything is the only way you learn; reading about it, or watching it, does nothing for you.

You are likely to have headaches as a recurring problem if you push yourself too hard, and you should watch your blood pressure too. Mars, ruling Aries, is a strong and forceful planet, and it is bound to get you a little over-stressed at times. You are also likely to have problems digesting things properly. Astrologically, all illnesses apply to your external condition as well as your internal condition, so think carefully; when your head aches you are banging it too hard against a problem which cannot be overcome that way, and when you are not digesting properly, you have not understood the implications of what you have taken on. In both cases, allow time to think and consider.

Taurus Ascendant

You were born in the middle of the morning if you have Taurus rising. Taureans are generally fond of food—did you arrive in time for morning coffee? You should have all the Taurean physical characteristics: quite thick-set, big around the neck and shoulders sometimes, and with large hands. You should have a broad mouth, and large eyes, which are very attractive.

You should also have a good voice—not only as a singing voice, but one which is pleasant to listen to in conversation too.

The Taurean method for getting things done is to look forward to, and then enjoy, the material reward for one's efforts. It is part of Taurean thinking that if you can't touch it, buy it, own it or eat it, it isn't real and it isn't worth much. You will also be concerned to keep what is yours, not to waste your energies on what won't gain you anything or increase your possessions, and not to attempt anything which you don't think you have more than a chance of achieving.

Taureans do have taste; not only taste for food, which they love, but artistic taste, which they develop as a means of distinguishing things of value which they would then like to acquire and gain pleasure from owning. Unlike the Capricorn way of doing things, which values quality because it is valued by others, Taureans enjoy their possessions for themselves. The drawback to the Taurean approach is the lack of enterprise, and the unwillingness to try things just for the fun of it.

Taurean Ascendant people have throat and glandular problems, and all problems associated with being overweight. They can also have back and kidney problems caused as a result of an unwillingness to let things go in their external life. A lighter touch is needed in the approach to problems of possession; shedding unwanted or outworn things in a desirable process.

Gemini Ascendant
If you have a Gemini Ascendant you were born somewhere in the late morning. You should achieve prominence in your chosen career simply by having the Sun so high in the sky when you were born. You should have expressive hands and a wide range of gestures which you use as you speak (ask your friends!) and you are perhaps a little taller than average, or than other members of your family. Gemini Ascendant people also have dark hair, if there is any possibility of it in their parents' colouring, and quick, penetrating eyes which flash with amusement and mischief; Gemini Ascendant women have very fine eyes indeed.

The Gemini approach to things, which you find yourself using, is one in which the idea of a thing is seen as being the most useful, and in which no time must be lost in telling it to other people so that they can contribute their own ideas and responses to the discussion. The performance of the deed is of no real importance in the Gemini view; somebody else can do that. Ideas and their development are what you like to spend time on, and finding more people to talk to, whose ideas can be matched to your own, seems to you to offer the most satisfaction.

There are two snags to the Gemini approach. The first is that there is a surface quality to it all, in which the rough outline suffices, but no time is spent in development or long-term experience. It may seem insignificant, but there is some value in seeing a project through to the end. The second snag is similar, but is concerned with time. The Gemini approach is immediate, in that it is concerned with the present or the near future. It is difficult for a Gemini Ascendant person to see farther than a few months into the future, if that; it is even more difficult for him to extend his view sideways in time to see the impact of his actions on a wider scene. Both of these things he will dismiss as unimportant.

Gemini Ascendant people suffer from chest and lung maladies, especially when they cannot communicate what they want to or need to, or when they cannot circulate socially in the way that they would like. They also have problems eliminating wastes from their bodies, through not realizing the importance of ending things as well as beginning them. In both cases, thinking and planning on a broader scale than usual, and examination of the past to help make better use of the future, is beneficial.

Cancer Ascendant
You were born in the middle of the day if you have your ascendant in Cancer and your Sun in Pisces. If you were born before noon, you should achieve prominence in your chosen career simply by having the Sun so high in the sky when you were born, as is sometimes the case with Gemini rising Pisceans, too. The

Cancerian frame, through which you project your energies, may mean that you appear rounder and less delicate than other Pisceans. Your energies are in no way diminished; in fact, you are likely to be even more determined to get things right. Your face could be almost cherubic, and you could have small features in a pale complexion with grey eyes and brown hair. The key to the Cancer frame is that it is paler than usual, less well defined than usual, and has no strong colouring. Strong noses and red hair do not come from a Cancerian ascendant.

The Cancerian approach to things is highly personal. All general criticisms are taken personally, and all problems in any procedure for which they have responsibility is seen as a personal failing. As a Piscean with a Cancerian way of working, you will be concerned to use your energies for the safe and secure establishment of things from the foundations up, so that you know that whatever you have been involved in has been done properly, and is unlikely to let you down in any way; you are concerned for your own safety and reputation. The other side of this approach is that you can be a little too concerned to make sure everything is done personally, and be unwilling to entrust things to other people. Not only does this overwork you, it seems obsessive and uncooperative to others.

The Cancer Ascendant person has health problems with the maintenance of the flow of fluids in his body, and a tendency to stomach ulcers caused by worry. Cancer Ascendant women should pay special attention to their breasts, since the affinity between the sign, the Moon as ruler of all things feminine, and that particular body system means that major imbalances in the life are likely to show there first. There could also be some problems with the liver and the circulation of the legs; the answer is to think that, metaphorically, you do not have to support everybody you know: they can use their own legs to stand on, and you do not have to feed them either.

Leo Ascendant
You were born in the afternoon if you have Leo as an Ascendant. Leo as the determinant of the physical characteristics makes

itself known by the Lion of the sign—you can always spot the deep chest, proud and slightly pompous way of walking, and more often than not, the hair arranged in some sort of man, either full, taken back off the face, and golden if possible. Leo ascendant people have strong voices and a definite presence to them. A Leo ascendant will bring to the fore any hereditary tendency to golden colouring, so reddish or golden hair, or a rosy complexion, may be in evidence, as will a heavy build in the upper half of the body.

The Leonine way of doing things is to put yourself in the centre and work from the centre outwards, making sure that everybody knows where the commands are coming from. It is quite a tiring way of working; you need to put a lot of energy into it, because you are acting as the driving force for everybody else. Preferred situations for this technique are those where you already know, more or less, what's going to happen; this way you are unlikely to be thrown off balance by unexpected develop- ments. The grand gesture belongs to the Leo method; it works best if all process are converted into theatrical scenes, with roles acted rather than lived. Over-reaction, over-dramatization, and over-indulgence are common, but the approach is in essence kind-hearted and well-meant. Children enjoy being with Leo Ascendant people, and they enjoy having children around them. The flaws in the approach are only that little gets done in difficult circumstances where applause and appreciation are scarce commodities, and that little is attempted that is really new and innovatory.

The health problems of the Leo Ascendant person come from the heart, and also from the joints, which suffer from mobility problems. These both come from a lifetime of being at the centre of things and working for everybody's good, and from being too stiff and unwilling to try and change in position. The remedy, of course, is to be more flexible, and to allow your friends to repay the favours they owe you.

Virgo Ascendant
A birth around sunset puts Virgo on the Ascendant. Physically,

this should make you slim and rather long, especially in the body; even if you have broad shoulders you will still have a long waist. There is a neatness to the features, but nothing notable; hair is brown, but again nothing notable. The nose and chin are often well-defined, and the forehead is often both tall and broad; the voice can be a little shrill and lacks penetration.

The Virgoan Ascendant person does not have an approach to life; he has a *system*. He analyses everything and pays a lot of attention to the way in which he works. It is important to the person with Virgo rising not only to be effective, but to be efficient; you can always interest them in a new or better technique. They watch themselves work, as if from a distance, all the while wondering if they can do it better. They never mind repetition; in fact they quite enjoy it, because as they get more practiced and more proficient they feel better about things. To you, being able to do things is everything, and unless you are given a practical outlet for your energies, you are completely ineffective. There is a willingness to help others, to be of service through being able to offer a superior technique, inherent in the Virgo way of doing things, which prevents Virgo rising people from being seen as cold and unfriendly. The problems in the Virgo attitude are a tendency to go into things in more detail than is necessary, and to be too much concerned with the 'proper' way to do things.

People with a Virgo Ascendant are susceptible to intestinal problems and may be prone to circulatory problems, and poor sight. All of these are ways in which the body registers the stresses of being too concerned with digesting the minutiae of things which are meant to be passed through anyway, and by not getting enough social contact. The remedy is to lift your head from your workbench sometimes, admit that the act is sometimes more important than the manner of its performance, and not to take things too seriously.

Libra Ascendant

You were born in the evening if you have Libra rising; it will give you a pleasant and approachable manner which will do a great deal to hide your anxieties and prevent people thinking anything but the best of you. You should be tallish, and graceful, as all Libra Ascendant people tend to be; they have a clear complexion, and blue eyes if possible, set in an oval face with finely formed features.

The Libra Ascendant person has to go through life at a fairly relaxed pace. The sign that controls his body won't let him feel rushed or anxious; if that sort of thing looks likely, then he will slow down a little until the panic's over. There is a need to see yourself reflected in the eyes of others, and so you will form a large circle of friends. You define your own opinion of yourself through their responses to you, rather than being sure what you want, and not caring what they think.

The drawback to the Libran approach is that unless you have approval from others, you are unlikely to do anything on your own initiative, or at least you find it hard to decide on a course of action. You always want to do things in the way which will cause the least bother to anyone, and to produce an acceptable overall result; sometimes this isn't definite enough, and you need to know what you do want as well as what you don't.

The Libran Ascendant makes the body susceptible to all ailments of the kidneys and of the skin; there may also be trouble in the feet. The kidney ailments are from trying to take all the problems out of life as you go along. Sometimes it's better to simply attack a few of the obstacles and knock them flat in pure rage—and in doing so you will develop adrenaline from the adrenal glands, on top of the kidneys!

Scorpio Ascendant

You were born towards midnight if you have a Scorpio Ascendant. A Scorpio Ascendant should give you a dark and powerful look, with a solid build, though not necessarily over-muscled. Scorpio Ascendant people tend to have a very penetrating and level way of looking at others, which is often disconcerting. Any possible darkness in the colouring is usually displayed, with dark complexions and dark hair, often thick and curly, never fine.

The Scorpio Ascendant person usually does things in a

controlled manner. He is not given to explosive releases of energy unless they are absolutely necessary; even then, not often. He knows, or feels (a better word, since the Scorpionic mind makes decisions as a result of knowledge gained by feeling rather than thinking), that he has plenty of energy to spare, but uses it in small and effective doses, each one suited to the requirements of the task at hand. It does not seem useful to him to put in more effort than is strictly necessary for any one activity; that extra energy could be used somewhere else. The idea that overdoing things for their own sakes is sometimes fun because of the sheer exhilaration of the release of energy does not strike a responsive chord in the Scorpio body, nor even much understanding. There is, however, understanding and perception of a situation which exists at more than one level. If anything is complicated, involving many activities and many people, with much interaction and many side issues which must be considered, then the Scorpio Ascendant person sees it all and understands all of it, in its minutest detail. They feel, and understand, the responses from all of their surroundings at once, but do not necessarily feel involved with them unless they choose to make a move. When they do move, they will have the intention of transforming things, making them different to conform to their ideas of how things need to be arranged.

Scorpio Ascendant people are unable simply to possess and look after anything; they must change it and direct it their way, and this can be a disadvantage.

Scorpio illnesses are usually to do with the genital and excretory systems; problems here relate to a lifestyle in which things are thrown away when used, or sometimes rejected when there is still use in them. It may be that there is too much stress on being the founder of the new, and on organizing others; this will bring head pains, and illnesses of that order. The solution is to take on the existing situation as it is, and look after it without changing any of it.

Sagittarius Ascendant
It would have been after midnight, probably, when you were

born for you to have a Sagittarius Ascendant. If you have, you should be taller than average, with a sort of sporty, leggy look to you; you should have a long face with pronounced temples (you may be balding there if you are male), a well-coloured complexion, clear eyes, and brown hair. A Grecian nose is sometimes a feature of this physique.

The Sagittarian Ascendant gives a way of working that is based on mobility and change. This particular frame can't keep still and is much more comfortable walking than standing, more comfortable lounging or leaning than sitting formally. You tend to be in a bit of a hurry; travelling takes up a lot of your time, because you enjoy it so. It is probably true to say that you enjoy the process of driving more than whatever it is that you have to do when you get there. You probably think a lot of your car, and you are likely to have one which is more than just a machine for transport—you see it as an extension, a representation even, of yourself. People will notice how outgoing and friendly you seem to be, but they will need to know you for some time before they realize that you enjoy meeting people than almost anything else, and you dislike being with the same companions all the time. There is a constant restlessness in you; you will feel that being static is somehow unnatural, and it worries you. You are an optimist, but can also be an opportunist, in that you see no reason to stay doing one thing for a moment longer than it interests you. The inability to stay and develop a situation or give long-term commitment to anything is the biggest failing of this sign's influence.

A person with Sagittarius rising can expect to have problems with his hips and thighs, and possibly in his arterial system; this is to do with trying to leap too far at once, in all senses. You may also have liver and digestive problems, again caused by haste on a long-term scale. The remedy is to shorten your horizons and concentrate on things nearer home.

Capricorn Ascendant
It must have been during the small hours of the morning when you were born for you to have a Capricorn Ascendant. This sign

often gives a small frame, quite compact and built to last a long time, the sort that doesn't need a lot of feeding and isn't big enough or heavy enough to break when it falls over. The face can be narrow and the features small; often the mouth points downwards at the corners, and this doesn't change even when the person smiles or laughs.

The Capricorn sees life as an ordered, dutiful struggle. There is a great deal of emphasis placed on projecting and maintaining appearances, both in the professional and the personal life; the idea of 'good reputation' is one which everybody with Capricorn rising, whatever their sun sign, recognizes at once. There is a sense of duty and commitment which the Sagittarian Ascendant simply cannot understand; here the feeling is that there are things which need doing, so you just have to set to and get them done. Capricorn Ascendant people see far forwards in time, anticipating their responsibilities for years to come, even if their Sun sign does not normally function this way; in such cases they apply themselves to one problem at a time, but can envisage a succession of such problems, one after another, going on for years.

The disadvantages of this outlook are to do with its static nature. There is often a sense of caution that borders on the paranoid, and while this is often well disguised in affluent middle-class middle age, it seems a little odd in the young. This tends to make for a critical assessment of all aspects of a new venture before embarking on it, and as a result a lot of the original impetus is lost. This makes the result less than was originally hoped in many cases, and so a cycle of disappointment and unadventurousness sets in, which is difficult to break. The Capricorn Ascendant person is often humourless, and can seem determined to remain so.

These people have trouble in their joints, and break bones from time to time, entirely as a result of being inflexible. On a small scale this can be from landing badly in an accident because the Capricorn Ascendant keeps up appearances to the very end, refusing to believe that an accident could be happening to him: on a large scale, a refusal to move with the times can lead

to the collapse of an outmoded set of values when they are swept
away by progress, and this breaking up of an old structure can
also cripple. They can get lung troubles, too, as a result of not
taking enough fresh air, or fresh ideas. The best treatment is to
look after their families rather than their reputation, and to think
about the difference between stability and stagnation.

Aquarius Ascendant

Having an Aquarius Ascendant means that you were born
before sunrise. This will make you more sociable than you would
otherwise have been, with a strong interest in verbal communication. There is a certain clarity, not to say transparency, about
the Aquarian physique. It is usually tall, fair, and well shaped,
almost never small or dark. There is nothing about the face
which is particularly distinctive; no noticeable colouring, shape
of nose, brows, or any other feature. It is an average sort of face,
cleanly formed and clear.

The person with an Aquarian Ascendant wants to be
independent. Not violently so, not the sort of independence tht
fights its way out of wherever it feels it's been put, just different
from everybody else. Aquarius gives your body the ability to do
things in ways perhaps not done before; you can discover new
techniques and practices for yourself, and don't need to stay in
the ways you were taught. There is a willingness to branch out, to
try new things; not a Scorpionic wish to make things happen the
way you want, but an amused curiosity which would just like to
see if things are any better done a different way. There is no need
for you to convince the world that your way is best: it only needs
to suit you.

Of course, an Aquarian needs to measure his difference
against others, and therefore you feel better when you have a
few friends around you to bounce ideas off, as well as showing
them how you're doing things in a slightly different way. You
function best in groups, and feel physically at ease when you're
not the only person in the room. You are not necessarily the
leader of the group; just a group member. Group leaders put their
energy into the group, and you draw strength and support from

it, so you are unlikely to be the leader, though paradoxically all groups work better for having you in them.

A handicap arising from an Aquarian Ascendant is that you are unlikely to really feel passionately involved with anything, and this may mean that unless you have support from your friends and colleagues you will be unable to muster the determination necessary to overcome really sizeable obstacles in your chosen career.

You are likely to suffer from diseases of the circulation and in your lower legs and ankles; these may reflect a life where too much time is spent trying to be independent, and not enough support is sought from others. You may also get stomach disorders and colds because you are not generating enough heat: get angrier and more involved in things!

Pisces Ascendant

You were born at sunrise if you have Pisces rising. Like Aries rising, Pisces is only possible as an Ascendant for about fifty minutes, so there aren't many of you around.

Pisces Ascendant people are on the small side, with a tendency to be a bit pale and fleshy. They are not very well co-ordinated and so walk rather clumsily, despite the fact that their feet are often large. They have large, expressive, but rather sleepy-looking eyes.

As a Piscean with Pisces rising, you will prefer to let things come to you rather than go out and look for them; you are likely to be more unsure than ever of your ability to cope with being yourself. Birth time is likely to be crucial; if you were born just after sunrise, you may find that you have no desire to live any kind of a public life at all, and as a consequence you be attracted to any sort of activity where you are either on your own or at least protected from the jostle of everyday living. If you were born before sunrise, you are likely to be a lot more confident about yourself, although you will still be almost painfully sensitive to criticism of any kind. You should be able to find yourself some sort of role to play that enables you to use your sensitivity at the same time as affording you some sort of protection from the harshness of others.

The major problem with a Pisces Ascendant is the inability to be active rather than reactive; you would rather be reacting to outside influences than generating your own movements from within yourself.

A Piscean Ascendant gives problems with the feet and the lymphatic system; this has connections with the way you move in response to external pressures, and how you deal with things which invade your system from outside. You may also suffer from faint-heartedness—literally as well as metaphorically. The remedy is to be more definite and less influenced by opinions other than your own.

6. Three Crosses: Areas of Life that Affect Each Other

If you have already determined your Ascendant sign from page 76, and you have read 'The Meaning Of The Zodiac' on page 11, you can apply that knowledge to every area of your life with revealing results. Instead of just looking at yourself, you can see how things like your career and your finances work from the unique point of view of your birth moment.

You will remember how the Ascendant defined which way up the sky was. Once you have it the right way up, then you can divide it into sectors for different areas of life, and see which zodiac signs occupy them. After that, you can interpret each sector of sky in the light of what you know about the zodiac sign which fell in it at the time that you were born.

Below there is a circular diagram of the sky, with horizon splitting it across the middle. This is the way real horoscopes are usually drawn. In the outer circle, in the space indicated, write the name of your Ascendant sign, not your Sun sign (unless they are the same, of course. If you don't know your time of birth, and so can't work out an Ascendant, use your Sun sign). Make it overlap sectors 12 and 1, so that the degree of your Ascendant within that sign is on the eastern horizon. Now fill in the rest of the zodiac around the circle in sequence, one across each sector boundary. If you've forgotten the sequence, look at the diagram on page 16. When you've done that, draw a symbol for the sun (☉—a circle with a point at its centre) in one of the sectors which has your Sun sign at its edge. Think about how far through the sign your Sun is; make sure that you have put it in the right sector. Whichever sector this is will be very important to you; having the sun there gives a bias to the whole chart, like the weight on one side of a locomotive wheel. You will feel that the activities of that sector (or house, as they are usually called) are most in keeping with your character, and you feel comfortable doing that sort of thing.

Make sure you have got your sums right. As a Pisces born in the afternoon, you might well have Leo rising, and the Sun in the 8th house, for example.

Now is the time to examine the twelve numbered sections of your own sky, and see what there is to be found.

Angular Houses: 1, 4, 7, 10

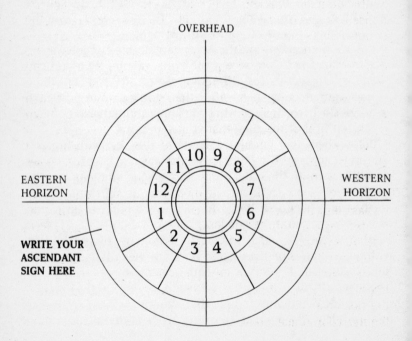

These are the houses closest to the horizon and the vertical, reading round in zodiacal sequence. The first house is concerned with you yourself as a physical entity, your appearance, and your health. Most of this has been dealt with in the section on Ascendants. If you have the Sun here, it simply doubles the impact of your Sun sign energies. Opposite to you is the seventh house, which concerns itself with everybody who is not you. Partners in a business sense, husbands, wives, enemies you are actually aware of (and who therefore stand opposed to you in plain sight) and any other unclassified strangers all belong in the seventh house. You see their motivation as being of the opposite sign to your Ascendant sign, as being something you are not. If you have Capricorn rising, you see them as behaving, and needing to be treated, which is perhaps more accurate, in a Cancerian manner. This is how you approach seventh house things. Use the keywords from 'The Meaning of the Zodiac' to remind yourself what this is. If you have the Sun in the seventh house you are your own best partner: you may marry late in life, or not at all. Perhaps your marriage will be unsuccessful. It is not a failure; it is simply that you are to a very great extent self-supporting, and have neither the ability nor the need to share yourself completely with another.

The whole business of the first and the seventh is to do with 'me and not-me'. For the personal energies of this relationship to be shown in tangible form, it is necessary to look at the pair of houses whose axis most squarely crosses the first/seventh axis. This is the fourth/tenth. The tenth is your received status in the world, and is the actual answer to the question 'What do you take me for?' No matter what you do, the world will find it best to see you as doing the sort of thing shown by the sign at the start of the tenth house. Eventually, you will start to pursue that kind of activity anyway, because in doing so you get more appreciation and reward from the rest of society. Your efforts in dealing with other, which is a first/seventh thing, have their result in the tenth, and their origins in the fourth. Where you came from is the business of the fourth. Expect to find clues there to your family, your home, the beliefs you hold most dear, and the eventual conclusion to your life (not your death, which is a different matter). If you have the Sun in the tenth, you will achieve some measure of prominence or fame; if your Sun is in the fourth, you will do well in property, and your family will be of greater importance to you than is usual.

There is, of course, some give and take between the paired houses. Giving more time to yourself in the first house means tht you are denying attention to the seventh, your partner; the reverse also applies. Giving a lot of attention to your career, in the tenth house, stops you from spending quite so much time as you might like with your family or at home. Spending too much time at home means that you are out of the public eye. There is only so much time in a day; what you give to one must be denied to the other.

This cross of four houses defines most people's life: self, partner, home and career. An over-emphasis on any of these is to the detriment of the other three, and all the arms of the cross feel and react to any event affecting any single member.

If these four houses have cardinal signs on them in your chart, then you are very much the sort of person who feels that he is in control of his own life, and that it is his duty to shape it into something new, personal, and original. You feel that by making decisive moves with your own circumstances you can actually change the way your life unfolds, and enjoy steering it the way you want it to go.

If these four houses have fixed signs on them in your chart, then you are the sort of person who sees the essential shape of our life as being one of looking after what you were given, continuing in the tradition, and ending up with a profit at the end of it all. Like a farmer, you see yourself as a tenant of the land you inherited, with a responsibility to hand it on in at least as good a condition as it was when you took it over. You are likely to see the main goal in all life's ups and downs as the maintenance of stability and enrichment of what you possess.

If these four houses have mutable signs on them in your chart, then you are much more willing to change yourself to suit circumstances than the other two. Rather than seeing yourself as the captain of your ship, or the trustee of the family firm, you see yourself as free to adapt to challenges as they arise, and if necessary to make fundamental changes in your life, home and career to suit the needs of the moment. You are the sort to welcome change and novelty, and you don't expect to have anything to show for it at the end of the day except experience. There is a strong sense of service in the mutable signs, and if you spend your life working for the welfare of others, then they will have something to show for it while you will not. Not in physical terms, anyway; you will have had your reward by seeing your own energies transformed into their success.

The Succedent Houses: 2, 5, 8, 11

These houses are called succedent because they succeed, or follow on from, the previous four. Where the angular houses define the framework of the life, the succedent ones give substance, and help develop it to its fullest and riches extent, in exactly the same way as fixed signs show the development and maintenance of the elemental energies defined by the cardinal signs.

The second house and the eighth define your resources; how much you have to play with, so to speak. The fifth and eleventh show what you do with it, and how much you achieve. Your immediate environment is the business of the second house. Your tastes in furniture and clothes are here (all part of your immediate environment, if you think about it) as well as your immediate resources, food and cash. Food is a resource because without it you are short of energy, and cash is a resource for obvious reasons. If you have the Sun here you are likely to be fond of spending money, and fond of eating too! You are likely to place value on things that you can buy or possess, and judge your success by your bank balance.

Opposed to it, and therefore dealing with the opposite viewpoint, is the eighth house, where you will find stored money. Savings, bank accounts, mortgages, and all kinds of non-immediate money come under this house. So do major and

irreversible changes in your life, because they are the larger
environment rather than the immediate one. Surgical operations
and death are both in the eighth, because you are not the same
person afterwards, and that is an irreversible change. If you have
the Sun in the eighth you are likely to be very careful with
yourself, and not the sort to expose yourself to any risk; you are
also not likely to be short of a few thousand when life gets tight,
because eighth house people always have some extra resource
tucked away somewhere. You are also likely to benefit from
legacies, which are another form of long-term wealth.

To turn all this money into some form of visible wealth you
must obviously do something with it, and all forms of self-
expression and ambition are found in the fifth and the eleventh
houses. The fifth is where you have fun, basically; all that you
like to do, all that amuses you, all your hobbies are found there,
and a look at the zodiac sign falling in that house in your chart
will show you what it is that you like so much. Your children are a
fifth-house phenomenon, too; they are an expression of yourself
made physical, made from the substance of your body and
existence, and given their own. If you have the Sun in the fifth
house you are likely to be of a generally happy disposition,
confident that life is there to be enjoyed, and sure that
something good will turn up.

The eleventh house, in contrast, is not so much what you like
doing as what you would like to be doing: it deals with hopes,
wishes, and ambitions. It also deals with friends and all social
gatherings, because in a similar manner to the Aries/Libra axis,
anybody who is 'not-you' and enjoying themselves must be
opposed to you enjoying yourself in the fifth house. If you have
the Sun in the eleventh house, you are at your best in a group.
You would do well in large organizations, possibly political
ones, and will find that you can organize well. You have well-
defined ambitions, and know how to realize them, using other
people as supporters of your cause.

The oppositions in this cross work just as effectively as the
previous set did: cash is either used or stored, and to convert it
from one to the other diminishes the first. Similarly, time spent

enjoying yourself does nothing for your ambitions and aims, nor does it help you maintain relationships with all the groups of people you know; there again, all work and no play . . .

If you have Cardinal signs on these four houses in your chart, then you think that using all the resources available to you at any one time is important. Although what you do isn't necessarily important, or even stable, you want to have something to show for it, and enjoying yourself as you go along is important to you. To you, money is for spending, and how your friends see you is possibly more important to you than how you see yourself.

Fixed signs on these four houses will make you reticent, and careful of how you express yourself. You are possibly too busy with the important things of life as you see them, such as your career and long-term prospects, to give much attention to the way you live. You feel it is important to have things of quality, because you have a long-term view of life, and you feel secure when you have some money in the bank, but you don't enjoy your possessions and friends for your own sake. You have them because you feel that you should, not because they are reason enough in themselves.

Mutable signs on these four houses show a flexible attitude to the use of a resource, possibly because the angular houses show that you already have plenty of it, and it is your duty to use it well. You don't mind spending time and money on projects which to you are necessary, and which will have a measurable end result. You see that you need to spend time and effort to bring projects into a completed reality, and you are willing to do that as long as the final product is yours and worth having. You are likely to change your style of living quite frequently during your life, and there may be ambitions which, when fulfilled, fade from life completely.

The Cadent Houses: 3, 6, 9, 12

The final four houses are called cadent either because they fall away from the angles (horizon and vertical axes), or because they fall towards them, giving their energy towards the formation of

ANGULAR HOUSES

SUCCEDENT HOUSES

CADENT HOUSES

the next phase in their existence. Either way, affairs in these houses are nothing like as firm and active as those in the other two sets of four. It may be useful to think of them as being given to mental rather than physical or material activities.

The third and ninth houses are given to thought and speech, with the ninth specializing in incoming thoughts, such as reading, learning and belief (religions of all kinds are ninth-house things), while the third limits itself to speaking and writing, daily chat, and the sort of conversations you have every day. If you have the sun in the third house, you will be a chatterbox. Talking is something you could do all day, and you love reading. Anything will do—papers, magazines, novels; as long as it has words in it you will like it. You will have the sort of mind that loves accumulating trivia, but you may find that serious study or hard learning is something that you cannot do.

The third house concerns itself with daily conversation, but the ninth is more withdrawn. Study is easy for a ninth-house person, but since all ideal and theoretical thought belongs here, the down-to-earth street-corner reality of the third house doesn't, and so the higher knowledge of the ninth finds no application in daily life. The third-ninth axis is the difference between practical street experience and the refined learning of a university. To give time to one must mean taking time from the other. If you have the Sun in the ninth, you are likely to hve a very sure grasp of the theory of things, and could well be an instigator or director of large projects; but you are unable to actually do the things yourself. Knowledge is yours, but practicality is not.

How this knowledge gets applied in the production of something new is a matter of technique, and technique is the business of the sixth house. The way things get done, both for yourself and for other people's benefit, is all in the sixth. Everything you do on someone else's behalf is there, too. If you have the Sun in the sixth house, you are careful and considerate by nature, much concerned to make the best use of things and to do things in the best way possible. Pride of work and craftsman-ship are guiding words to you; any kind of sloppiness is upsetting. You look after yourself, too; health is a sixth-house thing, and the Sun in the sixth sometimes makes you something of a hypochondriac.

Opposed to the sixth, and therefore opposed to the ideas of doing things for others, mastering the proper technique, and looking after your physical health, is the twelfth house. This is concerned with withdrawing yourself from the world, being on your own, having time to think. Energy is applied to the job in hand in the sixth house, and here it is allowed to grow again without being applied to anything. Recuperation is a good word to remember. All forms of rest are twelfth-house concepts. If you have the Sun in the twelfth house you are an essentially private individual, and there will be times when you need to be on your own to think about things and recover your strength and balance. You will keep your opinions to yourself, and share very little of your emotional troubles with anyone. Yours is most definitely not a life lived out in the open.

These houses live in the shadow of the houses which follow them. Each of them is a preparation for the next phase. If your Sun is in any of these houses, your life is much more one of giving away than of accumulation. You already have the experience and the knowledge, and you will be trying to hand it on before you go, so to speak. Acquisition is something you will never manage on a permanent basis.

If these houses have Cardinal signs on them in your chart, then preparation for things to come is important to you, and you think in straight lines towards a recognized goal. You will have firm and rather simplistic views and beliefs about matters which are not usually described in such terms, such as morality and politics, and you will be used to saying things simply and with meaning. Deception and half-truths, even mild exaggeration, confuse you, because you do not think in that sort of way.

If fixed signs occupy these houses in your horoscope, your thinking is conservative, and your mind, though rich and varied in its imagination, is not truly original. You like to collect ideas from elsewhere and tell yourself that they are your own. You rely on changing circumstances to bring you variety, and your own beliefs and opinions stay fixed to anchor you in a changing world; unfortunately, this can mean a refusal to take in new ideas, shown in your behaviour as a rather appealing old-fashionedness.

Having mutable signs on these houses in your horoscope shows a flexible imagination, though often not a very practical one. Speech and ideas flow freely from you, and you are quick to adapt your ideas to suit the occasion, performing complete changes of viewpoint without effort if required. You seem to have grasped the instinctive truth that mental images and words are not real, and can be changed or erased at will; you are far less inhibited in their use than the other two groups, who regard words as something at least as heavy as cement, and nearly as difficult to dissolve. Periods in the public eye and periods of isolation are of equal value to you; you can use them each for their best purpose, and have no dislike of either. This great flexibility of mind does mean, though, that you lack seriousness of approach at times, and have a happy-go-lucky view of the future, and of things spiritual, which may lead to eventual disappointments and regrets.

Houses are important in a horoscope. The twelve sectors of the sky correspond to the twelve signs of the zodiac, the difference being that the zodiac is a product of the Sun's annual revolution, and the houses are a product (via the Ascendant) of the Earth's daily revolution. They bring the symbolism down one level from the sky to the individual, and they answer the questions which arise when people of the same Sun sign have different lives and different preferences. The house in which the Sun falls, and the qualities of the signs in the houses, show each person's approach to those areas of his life, and the one which will be the most important to him.

Part 4

Pisces Trivia

7. Tastes and Preferences

Clothes

Pisceans are in many ways the luckiest people in the zodiac as far as dressing goes, because they can look wonderful in anything at all. The reason for this lies partly in the strong character of most modern clothes, and partly in the Piscean's ability to match his surroundings. If a certain jacket is supposed to give you an image of being, say, strong and slightly menacing, then a Piscean wearing it will look exactly like that, because he will faithfully absorb and reflect the image of the jacket. Somebody with a stronger and more identifiable personality may not suit it; his own personality may shine through and clash with the image of the jacket. In such cases we say that the jacket doesn't suit him. There are no clothes which don't suit a Piscean though; the designer's intentions become the wearer's, and the image is complete.

The disadvantage to this peculiar talent is that you can't *not* be affected by what you wear. When you throw on your coat to go out, you put on a whole new personality; the rest of us just grab something to keep us warm, usually the one we have left our keys in from last time. It also means that everybody you meet is going to react to you differently according to what you wear; it happens to everybody else as well, but the messages put out in your case are clearer and stronger because they are not mixed in with the wearer's own signals.

Perhaps to lessen the effect you have on others, or perhaps to express the diffuse nature of your planetary energies, you tend to choose clothes of indefinite shape. You don't usually like things which are very close-fitting, and you certainly don't like anything which restricts movement in any way. You may need to escape from a tricky situation at some stage: how can you do that if your clothes prevent you from moving? For the same reasons you don't like clothes which have angular lines and a severe cut: it all looks too definite to you, and you like things to be undefined wherever possible.

Female Pisceans usually have at least one dress which is made of many layers of floaty fabric. Floatiness is not a quality that many people would deliberately choose in their clothes, but it has a special appeal to Pisceans, as does semi-transparency. Any fabric light and fine enough to be one is usually the other as well, so you should have no trouble finding what you want.

A lot of a Piscean's favourite clothes look rather unfinished, if not frayed at the edges. It is probably to do with not wanting the definite-ness of a hem or a border—to Pisceans such things are restrictive boundaries.

All colours which change or shimmer are Piscean, as are all the colours of the ocean. That gives an enormous range of greens and blues, and it extends into mauves and purples too, because Pisces is at the far end of the zodiac as violet is at the far end of the rainbow of colours. Whichever colour you choose to wear, you are likely to choose a paler version of it than anybody else would. Anybody who is as sensitive to colour as you are doesn't need to shout all the time, after all. Pastels are intense enough for many Pisceans; they leave the stronger colours to the other signs.

The one area where you really indulge yourself is in your choice of shoes. Pisces as a sign is associated with the feet, remember, and your own may well be remarkable—either very large or very small. Many Pisceans like going barefoot whenever they can, because it makes their feet feel better. Shoes, though, are an obsession with you. You probably have dozens of pairs, in all colours and styles, for all occasions, and you still think that you don't have enough. Plenty of Pisceans carry a few spare pairs around with them in the car, in case their mood changes during the day and they need to wear something different on their feet.

Food and Furnishings

Pisceans eat fish, as you would expect, but their taste is wider than that. As always, the guiding principle is the emotional response, so you eat whatever appeals to you at any given moment, or anything which has a good feeling associated with it. You enjoy thick soups in winter, and ice-cream in summer. You enjoy birthday cake and Christmas cake not because the cake is good (though it usually is) but because of how happy everybody feels on such occasions. Jupiter, the planet behind the sign, will give you a taste for rich and spicy foods, which will surprise all those who think that you would like bland food to match your often pale complexion. Not so: food is something to be absorbed, and you would like the experience to be interesting and full of good associations. Association is the key to it all; if the food evokes a memory, a feeling, a mood, then you will like it. A Piscean home is somewhere soft and relaxing. There are no hard edges, and there are no formal arrangements. Furniture could be either very modern or very old, but it must evoke some sort of a mood, and it is likely to be soft and comfortable. The kind of home where hard straight chairs are formally arranged around a polished table is not Piscean. There is a lot of fabric in a Piscean home, arranged around things and over things, to round off edges and outlines, change the way the light falls, and generally add softness to the whole place. Ornaments and objects are not arranged or kept in any particular place, nor are they acquired because they match the furnishings or because of their value; they are all there because they have associations and memories for the owner, and that is their most important feature.

Hobbies

When a Pisces chooses to do something in his spare time it

usually contains movement, but not in a forceful way. It is usually a solitary activity, too, so that he can take some time off from the constant barrage of other people's emotional states. If he likes being outdoors, he will be drawn towards the ocean or the river, and may well enjoy sailing or fishing.

Lots of Pisceans like to project their accumulated experiences outwards, and turn to Arts and the theatre, either at an amateur level or semi-professionally. Pisceans make good painters—they have an understanding of the perceived image—but far more of them are photographers, probably for the same reasons.

A lot of Pisceans like to lose themselves in voluntary work, usually doing something to help at a local hospital or institution. They may be active on behalf of their local church; Pisces is the most spiritual of the signs.

Many Pisceans relax simply by looking at new and exciting images. Cinema is the great Piscean entertainment form, and so are television and video, but to a lesser extent. Finally, they listen to music and read books. Favourites are romances and travel books, because the images they create are so vivid; and so are books on astrology, because they show a world of meaning behind our actions, to which Pisceans are sensitive.

8. Piscean Luck

Being lucky isn't a matter of pure luck. It can be engineered. What happens when you are lucky is that a number of correspondences are made between circumstances, people, and even material items, which eventually enable planetary energies to flow quickly and effectively to act with full force in a particular way. If you are part of that chain, or your intentions lie in the same direction as the planetary flow, then you say that things are going your way, or that you are lucky. All you have to do to maximize this tendency is to make sure you are aligned to the flow of energies from the planets whenever you want things to work our way.

It is regular astrological practice to try to reinforce your own position in these things, by attracting energies which are already strongly represented in you. For Pisces, this means Jupiter, of course, and therefore any 'lucky' number, colour, or whatever for a Piscean is simply going to be one of those which corresponds symbolically with the attributes of Jupiter.

Jupiter's colour is blue, and the colours of Pisces itself are various greeny-blues, ocean colours, and sometimes violet; therefore a Piscean's lucky colours are these shades of blue, because by wearing them or aligning himself to them, for example by betting on a horse whose jockey's silks are turquoise blue, or supporting a sporting team whose colours include green and blue, he aligns himself to the energies of Jupiter and his sign, and thereby recharges the Solar energies that are already in him.

Pisces' preferred gemstone used to be an amethyst or a moonstone, but these days opals and pearls are often quoted too. Gemstones are seen as being able to concentrate or focus magical energies, and the colour of the stone shows its propensity to the energies of a particular planet. There are other stones quoted for the sign, such as turquoise and aquamarine; in most cases it is the colour which is the key.

Because Pisces is the twelfth sign, your lucky number is 12. Jupiter has its own number, which is 3, though some authorities quote 4 (but this doesn't matter, because 3 and 4 are both denominators of 12, which is the number of Pisces); that will be lucky for you too. All combinations of numbers which add up to 3 by reduction work the same way, so you have a range to choose from. Reducing a number is done by adding its digits until you can go no further. As an example, take 678: $6 + 7 + 8 = 21$, and then $2 + 1 = 3$. There you are—678 is a lucky number for you, so to buy a car with those digits in its registration plate would make it a car which, while you had it, you were very fond of, and which served you well.

Jupiter also has its own day, Thursday (jeudi in French, which is Jupiter's Day, yes?), and Pisces has a direction with which it is associated, the North-West. If you have something important to do, and you manage to put it into action on Thursday 3rd December (month number 12, remember), then you will have made sure that you will get the result best suited to you, by aligning yourself to your own planet and helping its energies flow unimpeded through you and your activity.

Jupiter also has a metal associated with it, and in the Middle Ages people wore jewellery made of their planetary metals for luck, or self-alignment and emphasis, whichever way you want to describe it. In the case of Pisces and Jupiter, that metal is tin. I know you are not likely to wear jewellery made of tin, though you might have a few little ornaments made of pewter, which is almost pure tin these days. The best planetary use of tin in regular use is probably a pewter tankard: all alcoholic beverages are Piscean, which you may not have known. Whether this is because they are digestible (Mutable) liquids, or because of the dream-like state they induce, is not clear. There are also plants for each planet, and foods too. Among Jupiter's plants are flowers like daisies and violets, fruits like gooseberries and raisins, and spices like cloves and nutmeg. There is almost no end to the list of correspondences between the planets and everyday items, and many more can be made if you have a good imagination. They are lucky for Pisceans if you know what makes them so, and if you believe them to be so; the essence of the process lies in linking yourself and the object of your intent with some identifiable token of your own planet, such as its colour or number, and strengthening yourself thereby. The stronger you are, then the more frequently you will be able to achieve the result you want—and that's all that luck is, isn't it?

A Final Word

By the time you reach here, you will have learnt a great deal more about yourself. At least, I hope you have.

You will probably have noticed that I appear to have contradicted myself in some parts of the book, and have repeated myself in others, and there are reasons for this. It is quite likely that I have said that your Sun position makes you one way, while your Ascendant makes you the opposite. There is nothing strange about this; nobody is consistent, the same the whole way through—everybody has contradictory sides to their character, and knowing some more about your Sun sign and your Ascendant will help you to label and define those contradictory elements. It won't do anything about dealing with them, though—that's your job, and always has been. The only person who can live your horoscope is you. Astrology won't make your problems disappear, and it never has been able to; it simply defines the problems more clearly, and enables you to look for answers.

Where I have repeated myself it is either to make the point for the benefit of the person who is only going to read that section of the book, or because you have a double helping of the energy of your sign, as in the instance of the Sun and Ascendant in the same sign.

I hope you found the relationships section useful; you may well find that the Sun-to-Ascendant comparison is just as useful in showing you how you fit in with your partner as the usual Sun-to-Sun practice.

Where do you go from here? If you want to learn more about astrology, and see how all of the planets fit into the picture of the sky as it was at your birth, then you must either consult an astrologer or learn how to do it for yourself. There is quite a lot of astrology around these days; evening classes are not too hard to find and there are groups of enthusiasts up and down the country. There are also plenty of books which will show you how to draw up and interpret your own horoscope.

One thing about doing it yourself, which is an annoyance unless you are aware of it in advance: to calculate your horoscope properly you will need to know where the planets were in the sky when you were born, and you usually have to buy this data separately in a book called an ephemeris. The reason that astrology books don't have this data in them is that to include enough for everybody who is likely to buy the book would make the book as big as a 'phone directory, and look like a giant book of log tables, which is a bit off-putting. You can buy ephemerides (the plural) for any single year, such as the one of your birth. You can also buy omnibus versions for the whole century.

So, you will need two books, not one: an ephemeris, and a book to help you draw up and interpret your horoscope. It's much less annoying when you *know* you're going to need two books.

After that, there are lots of books on the more advanced techniques in the Astrology Handbook series, also from the Aquarian Press. Good though the books are, there is no substitute for being taught by an astrologer, and no substitute at all for practice. What we are trying to do here is provide a vocabulary of symbols taken from the sky so that you and your imagination can make sense of the world you live in; the essential element is your imagination, and you provide that.

Astrology works perfectly well at Sun sign level, and it works perfectly well at deeper levels as well; you can do it with what you want. I hope that, whatever you do with it, it is both instructive and satisfying to you—and fun, too.

SUNS AND LOVERS

The Astrology of Sexual Relationships

Penny Thornton. It doesn't seem to matter how experienced –
or inexperienced – you are, when it comes to love and romance
there just *isn't* a fool proof formula. . . but this book does its best
to provide one! THE definitive astrological guide to sexual
relationships, this book is based upon the accumulated wisdom,
and observations of centuries of dedicated astrologists. Reveals:

- In-depth analysis of astrological types
- Male and female profiles for each star sign
- Zodiacal attitudes to intimate relationships
- Most compatible – and incompatible – partners

Each general star sign analysis is concluded with amazingly
frank reflections, often based upon personal interviews, with
many famous personalities including: Bob Champion; Suzi
Quatro; Colin Wilson; Jeremy Irons; HRH The Princess Anne;
HRH The Duke of York; Martin Shaw; Barbara Cartland; Twiggy
and many more. Written in an easy-to-read style, and packed
with illuminating and fascinating tit-bits, this book is compulsive
reading for anyone likely to have *any sort* of encounter with the
opposite sex!